tahoe blues

"Growing Up in the Tahoe Hood" by Tim Hauserman. An earlier version appeared in *Moonshine Ink*, July 2007. Copyright © 2007 by Tim Hauserman. Reprinted by permission.

"Seeing Blue" by Mojie Crigler. Excerpted from "Seeing Blue" which first appeared in the *Los Angeles Review*, Spring 2010. Copyright © 2010 by Mojie Crigler. Reprinted by permission of author.

"If the Unsuitable Neighbor Smells Snow" by Stefanie Freele. First published in *Foundling Review*, March 2010. Copyright © 2010 by Stefanie Freele. Reprinted by permission of author.

ISBN 978-1-936511-02-0

2012903090

Cover Art and Design: Charter Advertising/Design, Inc.
Special thanks to: Jim Hewitt, Chelsea De La Rosa, Courtney Berti
Copy Editor: Elisabeth Korb
Interior Design: Erin Bechtol
Printing and Binding: Thomson-Shore, Dexter, MI

Orders, inquiries, and correspondence should be addressed to:
      Bona Fide Books
      PO Box 550278, South Lake Tahoe, CA 96155
      (530) 573-1513
      www.bonafidebooks.com

tahoe blues

short lit on life at the lake

Editors
Kim Wyatt & Erin Bechtol

Bona Fide Books
Tahoe Paradise, CA

Contents

IV. Turquoise

V. Cobalt

VI. Ultramarine

VII. Sapphire

VIII. Slate

IX. Midnight

Lake Tahoe. Everyone has a story.

After seeing a collection of flash fiction and microessays about life in Alaska, I thought Tahoe needed a book like that too. I decided to gather true stories and fiction of no more than five hundred words and put them together, a literary mosaic of life at Lake Tahoe.

So I put out the call for submissions, and the stories came in from all around the lake: Tahoe City, Truckee, Incline Village, Meyers, Zephyr Cove, South Lake Tahoe, and beyond. This led to a cool discovery, an affirmation that we are not a bunch of separate hamlets, disconnected, but that we are one people magnetized by a big, blue body of water.

Some stories are straight-up fiction, others futuristic or post-apocalyptic. There are factual reminiscences, historic and otherwise, and portraits of colorful locals. Ghost stories and, of course, environmental yarns. But how to put all of this material together? The only choice that made sense to me was to group the pieces by shades of blue, arranged by theme, depth, and, sometimes, intangibles. *Tahoe Blues* alludes to jazz and all the different blue notes that make up the lake. And rather than make the distinction between fiction and nonfiction—both appear in the book, in roughly equal numbers—we thought we would leave it up to the reader to take away the truths therein.

Please enjoy this one-of-a-kind collection, crafted by Tahoe writers and those who just wanted to get their story down. Inside you'll find brief tales to savor in the lift line, at the beach, or in front of the wood-burning stove. I hope that the stories add a measure of clarity to the lake many of us call home.

Kim Wyatt
Publisher, Bona Fide Books

tahoe blues

short lit on life at the lake

I

powder blue

The little snowball is perched on the edge of the cliff. A bull's-eye at the exact point where I plan to take off. With a deep breath, I adjust my goggles and regrip my poles; my heart is racing.

I love this part.

Stabbing the poles into the snow, I push hard through my arms and step wide with my right ski. The only audible sound is the wind, and in this silence I feel completely alone. No one exists but me and that sinister little snowball. My speed increases as I transfer weight to my left ski then back to my right, the snowball growing larger and larger, grinning, taunting me, begging me to crush it beneath my feet. And I do.

With the snow-covered cliff and what remains of the snowball behind me, I take flight. Pulling my knees in to my chest, I thrust my arms forward, down the hill. I feel nothing, save for my heart pounding and the crisp winter air on my cheeks. I am weightless for what seems like an eternity, but somehow is never quite long enough. My eyes drift to the chosen landing zone: a pristine runway of untracked powder.

Gravity takes hold and pulls me back toward the earth. My skis skim the fresh snow, sinking deeper and deeper until finally I am no longer weightless. Pointing my tips at the untracked field ahead, I begin my quest for the perfect powder turn.

Just as I relax, my skis stop.

No warnings. Just stop.

My head goes down, my feet up.

The skis stay exactly where they are.

Somersaults ensue, one after the other. Down, down, down. Tiny crystals of Kirkwood powder fill my goggles, my mouth, my nose.

Finally the tumbling stops. I lift my head and pull off the snow-packed goggles. Gazing uphill at my stranded skis, I smile.

I love this part.

A Hike to Scott's Lake
Frank Riley

I thumbed through a hiking book, looking for an easy Tahoe hike. I didn't want to waste a cloudless summer afternoon indoors, but I wanted to watch the Giants play the Braves on TBS at 4:30. Found one: Scott's Lake. Only 2.7 miles, "a leisurely, gentle ascent," that should take only about an hour each way. Perfect, I thought.

So, I headed up Highway 89, found Big Meadow trailhead, and proceeded. Up. I mean, *up*. Not exactly Mount Everest *up*, but ascending four hundred feet in less than half a mile translated into a lot of "I-didn't-dream-it'd-be-this-tough" couch potato elevation gain.

I thought about going back, but surrounded by blue sky, brown mountains, green trees… hey, that's why I moved to Tahoe from the Bay Area in the first place. So, I carried on.

And it was a pretty little hike. There were some nice panoramic views of purple mountains, blue sky, and green trees, with babbling streams and chirping birds thrown in. The book said that if you want to get away from people, Scott's 2.7 miles is as isolated as they come in the Tahoe Basin. So I had it all to myself. And, sometimes, you know, all you really need is sky, mountains, trees, streams, and birds to make you think that maybe, just maybe, it's worth putting up with all those casino jerks and dead-end dates, just to be able to drink in all that nature stuff.

So, it came as a bit of a shock when, approaching a narrow pass flanked by a lofty hillside and a thick grove of trees, I heard a peculiar huffing sound. Puzzled, I came around the bend. My first thought was, "Why is that massively heavy man wearing a fur coat and running right at me on all fours?" My second thought was, "Argggggg!" My third thought was, "Argggggg! A bear!"

tahoe blues

Because, yes, it was one of nature's shaggy brown-furred own, weighing in at a million billion pounds, maybe two hundred feet away. My hiking must have irritated his own sense of nature, because the huge brown organic freight train was coming straight at me.

Moments like that are odd. You don't pray. You don't scream. You don't see your life flash past. You stand—stock still—becoming one with every deer in the world who had ever watched an on-coming Volkswagen rush dead straight ahead.

The path was too narrow. The mountain and trees were in the way. There was no place to go. Except to the Great Beyond. I braced for impact.

And then the bear stopped. Just stopped. As if surprised I was there. He looked at me. Sniffed. And then, nonchalantly, turned around and padded away.

I stared. And I blinked. And I remembered to breathe.

In that brief encounter, I realized two things. One, that my belief in miracles just got a big boost. And, two, if I could sell breath mints to bears, I'd make a fortune.

WOMEN'S MOUNTAIN FASHION
Margaret Elysia Garcia

To live in the mountains is to lose all sense of fashion. The mountains require that women, for the most part, surrender all notions of femininity in the flatland below. As you climb in elevation you lose tights, heels, skirts, dresses, makeup, earrings hanging down more than an inch. By the time you've arrived at your destination you've adopted the dress code: middle-aged social worker or lesbian or perhaps single mom of twenty years or plain-clothed nun. We mountain women seriously think of investing in stock ownership of Land's End or Patagonia. We wear warm, androgynous turtlenecks and sensible shoes with a sole for rock climbing. More than likely our fashion statement becomes which make and color of truck to purchase and whether the dog in the back of the cab is going to be a golden retriever, a husky, or a black lab. And this is regardless of sexual preference.

Women of the mountains and lake get their nails done, eyebrows waxed, and legs shaved—but only if they are leaving town. If a given woman has all three of these things accomplished she's either just returned from a vacation, is on her way down to the coast, or is entertaining friends from out of the area. We've accepted a level of hairiness; for each other, we sport unibrows. We have no one to impress, and hair is an extra layer of warmth, like silk long johns only furrier. It's as natural and commonplace as fake boobs in Los Angeles. Only for complete strangers who will probably barely smile at us on planes do we wax and pluck.

When I first arrived here, I was determined to keep my fashion sensibilities. I was raised by a lesbian with fourteen turtlenecks in her closet, so nonfunctional clothing has always been my rebellion. I resist the temptation to fold into function. I wear V-neck sweaters. I wear dresses. I wear heels with Fluevog or Steve Madden traction. I wear clothes I would have worn in San Francisco or Los Angeles. In trendier places, I might go unnoticed, having just risen to the level of basic fashion expectations. I wear a longer wool coat. I've added more gloves and scarves. In the land of sweatshirts with bubble paint and caked cowboy boots and Wranglers, I am queen. I get ready for work dressed in a long black dress and 1930s hat with black pumps and a bright coral scarf and long earrings. In the kingdom of the blind, the one-eyed man is king. In the mountains, I'm a runway model.

There's a woman that wears stripper heels to pick her son up from elementary school. Rain or shine, that thirty-year-old, stay-at-home mother of two is wearing clear, four-inch stripper heels. Anywhere else she'd just look like a whore. Up here, she looks like a goddess.

MOUNTAIN WOMAN
Suzanne Stone

Let's begin on the trail to Meiss Meadow. June and I are hiking in the high mountains of the Lake Tahoe Basin. You will see that June is in touch with all that surrounds us: the animals, even the rocks.

At a junction, we take the path to Meiss Lake around the far side where there is access to boulders above the water. Here we stop for lunch. A few squirrels gather round us looking for a handout.

"How is your life here in Meiss Meadow?" June asks the closest squirrel.

"Oh, the winter was hard?" she answers.

As she talks quietly with the squirrels, little birds begin to drift in, chickadees and others. She addresses several of these individuals as they draw closer. Soon we are completely surrounded by small creatures.

Lulled by June's voice, I lie back on a tuft of grass gazing at the blue sky. Next, June talks to the rocks. They tell her of their long ages here in this beautiful meadow, wearing away with the wind and the snow, the waters melting and rushing over them. I say to myself, "That's remarkable! She's talking to the rocks."

In her forties, tall and thin with brown hair, brown eyes, and pale skin, June is not remarkable in appearance or profession. To support her twin boys, she works as a bookkeeper. However, she is known in our area for her way with animals. She once helped me with my two cats. Missy would not let her son, Tom, come into the house. His habit was to empty the food bowl each time he entered. June convinced Missy and Tom to share—a remarkable accomplishment. However, I digress.

Let's go back to the trail. After lunch as June and I walk out of the valley, bells begin to ring in the distance—cowbells, like a symphony growing in intensity.

tahoe blues

"I haven't heard or seen cows in the meadow for some time," I remark to June.

"Yes, they are still here," she answers. "They want to be heard."

The bonging and tinkling accompanies us up the trail until we pass the cow pond, leaving Meiss Meadow, "the center of the world."

I lost touch with June after she moved to Stockton in the late '90s. However, I did hear in the news that she ran for mayor of the city and lost by a very narrow margin.

Although I have changed June's name for privacy, this is a true story. Doesn't it lift your spirits?

Perhaps you think I was dreaming after lunch as June talked on and on with the squirrels and the birds and the rocks. But remember the cowbells. I was awake and walking then.

FROM THE HILDINGER LOG
Jim Hildinger

The following was written by my dad at Angora Lake during the winter of 1937–38.

Saturday, January 15, 1938

It was on the tenth of January that this thing all started. We were sitting on the front porch basking in the hot sun at Los Gatos when the post-man came swinging down the street. In our mail we got we got a little white envelope with a "Camp Richardson – Lake Tahoe, California" postmark on it with a return to Ann Nickelson up in the corner. I'll let you read it. After "Dear Bill and Effie and the boys" it goes on to tell about the parties they have been having up here and that instead of the storms bringing snow, so far they have brought rain and warm weather. In fact, so much warm weather that the ice started to move down the river and out into Lake Tahoe so that all the men folks of the district couldn't cut their summer's supply of ice. Then it went on to say that "I think you could make it up to your place if you wanted to come in at this time." Now, really I can't tell you any more of what was in that letter. I think that was about as far as we read. It just seemed that those few magic words were all that were necessary to get us started and finally set us down here in this comfortable chair taking another little sip of this fine Port which sure puts a big smile all across one's face. Well, so much for the letter. We didn't ask each other whether we were going to go. We didn't do any consulting. Next thing we knew each of us had made up a list of those things which had to be purchased and done so that we would arrive here in good condition. Albert had to have some goulashes, Mother some shoes, the car greased, Jimmie's snowshoes had to have some new leather thongs and so, late that night, we had about finished packing. Twelve apple boxes, two dunnage sacks, one large gunny sack of walnuts, several suitcases, and the odds and ends of footballs, toys, my cameras and it seemed a million other things were ready to be packed in the car and the trailer.

Six weeks later...

In twenty-two days and nights of continuous storm and during several smaller subsequent storms sixty-four feet of snow fell making a record solid pack of sixteen (16) feet on the level. Our houses were buried. We were a bit alarmed—the phone line broke—and it kept on snowing—but at last (May) spring came. We were glad—both for the winter and for the spring.

Signed — AW Hildinger

CONVERSATION WITH A BEAR
Steve Shilstone

While strolling through the woods on the way to Nevada Beach, I met a bear. The following took place.

ME: Hey, bear.

BEAR: Hey, man.

ME: What you doin' in this neck of the woods?

BEAR: I was about to ask you the same question. Me being a bear and all, I more or less belong here.

ME: Well, yeah, I guess.

BEAR: You got anything to eat?

ME: Not really, just this candy bar wrapper.

BEAR: Hand it over.

ME: Sure. Have a party.

BEAR: Is that supposed to be funny?

ME: Not at all, not at all. Just enjoy… with my blessings.

BEAR: You got somethin' against eatin' garbage?

ME: Me? No, not me. I practically live on tortilla chips.

BEAR: Yeah? Where's your house?

ME: (lying) Mine? Oh… far… hundreds of miles. Next to a big city. In it, actually.

BEAR: Next time you come to Tahoe, bring me a bag of tortilla chips.

ME: Right. Yeah. Sure thing. Have to be going now. Bye.

BEAR: And no spicy. I don't like spicy.

ME: (hurrying off) No spicy. Hate spicy. Me too. Spicy bad.

BEAR: (muttering) Dipwad.

II

cerulean

Lost on Migration?
Elisabeth Korb

Birds follow fairly set paths of migration, typically ones of a north-to-south range, and mammals tend to stick to their unmarked territory lines. An ornithologist would surely drop his thousand-dollar binoculars upon spotting a brown thrasher at Lake Tahoe. *Squawk?!* Georgia's state bird wouldn't dream of crossing the spine of the Rockies for a vacation, let alone a full-fledged relocation. Yet in 2004, after twenty-one years of living in the South, I defied range, territory, and home to move more than two thousand miles west, to a place I'd only seen in ink and pixels.

While I think of myself as an atypical Tahoe resident, I'm certainly not as out of place here as a brown thrasher would be. In fact, the untrained eye wouldn't have a clue about my origins. Any trace of a twang was lost in my English studies. I instinctively eschewed colloquialisms, as if I knew I would leave them all behind.

Goodbye humidity, farewell sweet, sweet tea. Good riddance tanning beds and strip malls and "hikes" that involved meandering concrete. I belonged here, out West, in Tahoe. Humidity was nonexistent; buildings didn't scrape at the sky. Fences became Mother Nature's doing: tall, glopping snowbanks melting in layers like forgotten tiramisu. Friends were heroic versions of my outdoorsy self: flawless, strong characters doing it all faster, higher, and with way more abandon.

As my new companions showed me the way up peaks, down singletrack, and across water, my outdoor prowess was recast as naïveté. I thought I was a ripping snowboarder until I learned that Tahoe locals rarely used groomed trails. I thought I could handle a mean snowstorm until I moved to the West Shore and the flakes piled up foot upon foot, month after month. I bought a snowblower.

I thought I could conquer any sport until I experienced how much pain and mental discipline came with most alpine pursuits: roughed-up, skin-scraped fingers taking my mind off the fun, high-elevation everything unearthing my fears, jabbing at my asthmatic lungs in a triumphant "go back to sea level!" Is adrenaline still my friend?

I'm now learning to embrace the dichotomy of being what you call a "wuss" in these parts and a "daring adventurer" in Atlanta. I sometimes contemplate yet another move, to land me somewhere in the middle. But does feeling at home have to mean fitting in?

A biologist friend told me he recently spotted Oklahoma's state bird at the outlet of the Upper Truckee River. He's even seen brown thrashers on the California coast. "Lost birds on migration," he called them. Maybe they weren't lost at all.

I often think about the rare, solitary wolverine first captured on a researcher's camera north of Truckee four years ago. He's still here, far from where biologists say he ought to be. Does he realize that distance from others of his kind? Or to that would he reply, "What kind?" And just live voraciously.

You Don't Seem Like You're from Tahoe
Krista Lukas

Well, I am. My parents met at Heavenly in 1968. Dad came over as one of a posse of Austrians recruited to teach skiing; Mom was on spring break from San Jose State. She took a group lesson and charmed him with her wit and flamboyance. He was shy, still learning English, and all ears for her stories. Weeks later, she moved up and started dealing blackjack at Harveys, finished her degree by correspondence. They lived in an apartment off Pioneer Trail. After adventures in Mexico and Europe, they married at the Carson City courthouse, had dinner at the Top of the Wheel, and moved to Mom's family-owned resort motel on the North Shore, serving as live-in manager, housekeeper, groundskeeper, building maintenance engineer, garbage collector, late-night desk clerk, and early-morning wake-up caller. They tell me I was conceived during a weekend trip to Las Vegas, born forty weeks later at Tahoe Forest Hospital. And there we were, a family by the accident of a ski lesson turned romantic.

Dad equates the motel years to living in a minimum-security prison, although it was a perfect environment for raising kids. Home every day, he prided himself on knowing his babies well enough to discern our various cries rather than being an only-back-for-dinner-and-bedtime kind of father. We started skiing when I was four and my sister only two. I've asked my dad if he ever dreamed of one of us becoming an Olympic racer since he, having grown up in a town that lacked a chairlift, missed his chance at the same. Did he ever wish for me to carry that out? "No," he says. "I knew skiing wasn't your thing when I put you in a race and you snowplowed past the finish line sucking your thumb."

tahoe blues

I had to be dragged skiing, but you couldn't tear me away from books. And learning cursive in third grade was my ticket to writing faster. I'll never forget that afternoon riding home on the school bus when I could finally decode "Fire Lite" in its ornate script above the lobby door of a motel down the street from ours. Reading and writing may be what turned me into someone who surprises people simply by being from Tahoe. "You seem too sophisticated," they say, "too cosmopolitan." What? I'm from a place people visit and move to from all over the world. I've never asked *what* exactly is so surprising, but I wonder, is it something about the way I talk? My taste in fiction, theater, Asian cuisines? The fact that my radio is tuned to NPR? They seem to think they're paying me a compliment, but I'm not flattered. It's backhanded at best. Where am I supposed to be from, back east? The city? I'm from Lake Tahoe, from somewhere famous and beautiful. My parents met in a place named for heaven.

Fishing with Charo
Mark Maynard

When she first descended the Sand Harbor boat ramp where my father and I were waiting at the dock, I was disappointed. Her red hair was hidden beneath an Audrey Hepburn head scarf; a pair of oversized sunglasses covered most of her face. Where I'd imagined there'd be a cleavage-revealing ruffled flamenco blouse, there was a button-down windbreaker. I actually began to doubt that the petite woman holding a little boy's hand was indeed the famous queen of "Cuchi-Cuchi" until she greeted my father in a clipped Spanish chirp.

"Hey-lo An-dee!"

Charo and her husband, Kjell—a tall, handsome Swede—had been talking with my father for months about building a house in Incline Village. When they told him they'd be in town with their seven-year-old son, my dad offered to take them all fishing.

If they were surprised the five of us would be piling into our twenty-five-year-old, fourteen-foot aluminum boat, they showed no outward signs. Charo's young son, Shel, seemed particularly excited. We carefully embarked, and Dad gunned the outboard *Evinrude* as we made our way on the sparkling waters of the East Shore.

As any Tahoe local knows, it is always the lake that takes center stage. In the early eighties, we Incliners practiced undemonstrative brushes with celebrity. We shopped for produce at Raley's with Mr. Spock, drove past Ben Cartwright walking along Lakeshore Drive, and sat next to Peter Graves (known to my parents from the television show *Mission Impossible* but recognizable to me only as the pilot from the movie *Airplane*) at Jake's on the Lake. Our famous neighbors were to be left untouched and enjoyed as part of the local scenery—just like the deer and coyotes.

tahoe blues

The trout were a different story, however. This is what we were after with the world's foremost classical guitarist and her family. We hovered above tourmaline and indigo shoals. Waves slapped the aluminum bow, the bubbling and gurgling lulling the conversation to a stage whisper just loud enough to be heard over the sputtering of the ancient motor.

The only thing we pulled out of the lake that day were Shelito's sunglasses after he'd leaned over the side to gauge the depth of a looming boulder that looked as if it would breach the hull, Titanic-like, only to have us glide more than ten feet above it.

When we approached the dock with an empty creel, I felt bad that my father and I had failed our Hollywood clientele. As we clambered back up on the dock, another local fisherman, obviously not recognizing one of *The Love Boat*'s most frequent passengers as she disembarked from our dinghy, asked what we'd caught.

The answer, or perhaps the voice that gave it, left him speechless on the dock.

"We caught a *beeg chark*!"

Our guests were thrilled. I'd forgotten the power of Tahoe's presence on one's mood. How its calming waters can soothe even the worldliest travelers—fish or no fish.

TRUCKEE RIVER RAFTING
Brittany Michelson

Once you drive across Fanny Bridge, you reach the launching point of the Truckee River Rafting Company. My brother and I always laugh at the name of this bridge. Out the window, we see a line of backsides along the railing, as people lean out over the rushing water of the dam. Dad told us that this historic Tahoe City bridge received its name from all the fannies seen from the road. This viewing spot on Tahoe's northwest side is the lake's only outlet.

I count fourteen butts, all sizes, leaning over the bridge. There is a classic postcard of this famous line of fannies. I once bought one for a quarter in a souvenir shop in Truckee, and my brother and I couldn't stop laughing.

After Dad parks the car near the river raft company, I race to the bridge. Down below, the green and turquoise water swirls like tie-dyed paint, with a frothy white top that reminds me of bubble bath. The river sweeps under the bridge, its roar drowning out talking and traffic. I lean over to catch the spray on my tongue.

Rafting on the Truckee River is a two- to three- hour adventure that ends at the River Ranch Restaurant. The ride is only three miles—a tiny fraction of the whole river, which is 120 miles long.

Soon, we have orange paddles and vests and are seated in a yellow rubber raft—Dad at the front, my brother and I in the middle, and Mom in the back. Two tanned, muscled workers push our raft away from the dock, and we are instantly swept along. It is exhilarating and unnerving at the same time, being moved and lifted across the rapids. At the start, the current is swift so we relax and let the river do the work. When the icy water shoots into our faces, my brother and I scream as if we're running through sprinklers. If

tahoe blues

the raft turns to the side, Dad and Mom stick their oars in and draw them through the water until we are facing downstream again.

Truckee River rapids are class one and two, so we don't encounter anything harrowing, but to us, it feels like we're rafting down the Amazon. There are a few points where we are moving so fast it's as if the raft could lift off the river. My stomach flips a time or two.

"Duck!" Dad yells, and I flatten on the bottom of the raft to miss a mountain laurel branch stretching across an eddy.

"Criminy!" Mom shrieks when the raft gets stuck on a large rock and the four of us have to work as a team to dislodge it.

Then we are gliding down the smooth parts, full of wonder and trust in the river and thinking of the juicy burgers that await us at the River Ranch.

THE WHITE LADY OF SAWMILL POND
Duane Wallace

Sawmill Pond is a scary place. It is located a couple of miles outside of the city limits heading toward Tahoe Paradise. The story goes that there used to be a sawmill at the pond. A beautiful young woman was set to marry a young man who worked for the mill. She had found a stunning white wedding gown. As fate would have it, on the day of her wedding the mill caught fire, killing all the workers including her betrothed. The girl lost her mind. She rode to the mill in her wedding dress and then tragically ended her own life among the ruins and ashes. From then on, sightings were reported of a young woman in a white wedding dress accompanied by the fog that hangs over the pond, especially at night. Some say that if you are driving past you might look in your rearview mirror and see the woman sitting in the backseat of your car, or see her floating through the mist searching for her fiancé.

At times, especially around Halloween, I would tell this story to my nieces and nephews and then drive them out to the pond. There was usually a slight or heavy fog hanging in the air. I would stop the car, and pretend that it wouldn't start. The kids would scream and beg me to start the car and get away—then they would ask me to do it again. I continued the spooky fun with my own children as they grew up. They loved the excitement even in their teens.

One night around midnight, I got a call that my business's burglar alarm had gone off. As I drove past the pond, it was unusually foggy. The water was shrouded in a heavy mist. Unbelievably, as I rolled past I saw a chilling sight—a white form bobbing around, a good ten feet up in the air. I caught my breath and drove past, dreading the return trip. What on earth could it have been?

A half hour later, I was on my way back home feeling anxious. There it was again! I slowed down and peered through the fog. I was not willing to let the mystery get the best of me. Then the fog drifted away to reveal a young woman dressed in white, wearing a white cowboy hat and riding a tall white horse. She bobbed and swayed as the horse walked along the side of the road. To this day, I wonder why a young woman would be riding alone in the dark of night at Sawmill Pond.

At least I had solved the mystery. *Or had I?*

We Chose Lightning
Meghan Robins

At fourteen years old, I was highly out-motivated, out-ranked, and out-paced by my dad and two sisters as we ended our fifth day hiking in Desolation Wilderness. Taking up the rear had become my pastime, and the expectation of camping at a river two easy downhill miles away was all that provoked my tired legs. As we made what should have been our final descent, we kicked ourselves for thinking we could find a place that the mosquitos would not. There they were. Waiting. Licking their metaphorical lips, their tiny insect feet rubbing together like Mr. Burns whispering, "Mmmm… excellent."

Deafened by that sickening buzz of bloodsuckers, blinded by hands furiously swatting exposed skin, our walk turned to a run as we dashed up and down the riverside searching for a place to cross the surging rapids. Our packs clanked against our backs, branches scratched our faces and tousled our hair, we ran like unabashed crazy people through the woods. Every moment counted, for every mosquito was calling in cruel and unnecessary reinforcements.

A quarter mile off trail we found a sapling lying across a shallow part of the river, branches akimbo. Hillary attempted to cross it, but turned around halfway. Dad took the direct route, lunging through the rapids, soaking himself to the bone. Emily and I watched in horror. The bugs were closing in—were already in— our clothes, our socks, our hair. We jumped into the river, dragging ourselves to the other side. Wet, tired, and swollen, we ran against an army of incorrigible insects. Twenty minutes of gut-wrenching endurance, and we were at the top of a saddle where we stopped to contemplate our next predicament.

tahoe blues

With two huge granite knolls pillared on either side, the only flat space to camp for two miles in any direction was the trail on which we stood. But only when the breeze briefly parted the blinding clouds of insects did we notice the runoff stream trickling down the middle of it. Then, over the maddening mosquito buzz we heard the chilling roar of thunder.

A quick vote: bugs or lightning? Unanimously, we chose lightning. We scampered up the granite as the skies unleashed, barely giving us time to set up our tents beside a tree with charcoaled scars running down its crippled spine. In nervous silence we counted lightning strikes within a mile. Had we really chosen death over annoyance?

Two deafening hours of rain, thunder, and lightning later, the darkness of the storm retreated, and radiant oranges, reds, and pinks filled the sky, knocking us over as we emerged from our tents. We had run through purgatory, suffered beasts and tempests, and were rewarded with the most beautiful Sierra sunset any of us had ever seen. We stood atop that granite knoll, fifty miles from anywhere, staring into heaven, not a buzz of bugs or a crack of thunder. Just the quiet.

CRAWDAD FISHING
Brittany Michelson

You're a wiry kid, freckle-faced and curious, and you're crawdad fishing at the end of a wooden pier that extends off the shore into North America's largest alpine lake, located along the border between California and Nevada. With a depth of 501 meters, Lake Tahoe is the second deepest lake in the United States, next to Crater Lake in Oregon.

You're on your stomach with your legs stretched out behind you, holding a string with a piece of raw bacon tied to the end, dangling in the water. It is the summer of 1990, and one of the worst drought periods Tahoe has had. The lake is so shallow you can see the sandy bottom from the pier. You are eight and not very tall, and when you walk into the water it is only waist high.

Your brother is next to you, also stretched on his stomach, his string and bacon dangling in the water next to yours. Your arms and legs are the color of pennies. The lake is a still, luminescent postcard, except for the occasional Jet Ski or boat with a distant hum like the buzzing of bees. You pull your string out of the water and set it on the pier, the piece of bacon dripping wet. Turning on your back, you search the sky for a single puff of cloud, but there is not even a dusting of strata. The hot, uneven planks of wood support you. Every part of you is alive in the presence of the lake.

You remember the crawdads and turn back over, drop your string in, and watch the water for movement.

"There's one on my bacon!" your brother shouts. "He's grabbing on."

"Pull him up quick before you lose him, but be careful that he doesn't fall off," you instruct.

tahoe blues

He pulls his line up and a brownish-orange crawdad the length of your foot is attached to the end, his bendy legs gripping the bacon. Your brother sets the string on the pier and you lean down to get a good look. He's a strange creature, and you are fascinated. His shell glistens—rainbow colors on a shiny surface. He moves his spindly legs on the bacon. Your brother picks him off by the shell and sticks him in your face. You scream and jump back, and he laughs, tossing the crawdad into the water.

"See ya, wouldn't want to be ya!" he yells across the lake, the echo traveling back like a boomerang.

Then the two of you lie back down, completely still, and press your stomachs into the hot wood, as if you might disappear into the postcard.

III

aquamarine

WHAT I THINK ABOUT WHEN I WAX MY SKIS
Mary Cook

I

I pepper the base of my skis with hot drops of wax the size of dimes. "My skis are crying," I joke. When flattened, the wax beads swell to the size of nickels, losing value. Isn't that funny? Dimes exist as the oddball of the American money family. I think of other instances when something smaller can mean something greater.

II

The iron hisses and crackles as I smooth each mound of wax, one pooling into another, and another. This is what I want: a pond of melted wax. I think of an ice rink Zamboni as I drive the iron, slow and methodical, along the entire length of my ski, until the pools glide and harden into a clean pane.

III

The iron smokes, too hot to touch, and I turn its dial from "Cotton" to "Silk." I think of lovers, their thighs burning between satin sheets. I imagine them dripping hot wax onto each others' stomachs, scripting their initials maybe, or polka-dot hearts. And they squeeze each dollop off with their teeth.

IV

I think of 1950s housewives and modern-day Martha Stewarts. And their disgruntled counterparts, the Betty Friedans and the Maureen

tahoe blues

Dowds. It's true, whether a political crusader or a domestic dame, all women press and starch and blow steam. I can't remember the last time I ironed clothes.

V

I think of my high school English teacher and her long curly hair. She wore it wet like a mop. One day she told me, as she fingered my flat mane, that she used to iron her hair every morning on an ironing board. She did this when she was my age—back and forth for an hour, just to look like someone else.

VI

And I think of my mother, born and raised in Vermont. She used to ski, carving Ss at Killington and Stowe, but stopped when she had kids. Or perhaps she quit when she married and moved to New York. Either way, she traded wax for onesies, for a husband, for me, each just as moldable and malleable as the next.

SCRAPED CLEAN
Charlotte Austin

I came to Lake Tahoe for two reasons: to spend quiet days with the man I love, and to remember how to write. There's an openness here that I crave, a sense of being scraped clean by the dry blue sky.

On my first morning alone, I crammed my feet into the frozen shoes I'd left outside overnight and went for a walk in the meadow with Ruby, the neighborhood stray. She pranced at my side, barking when I got too serious.

Because I am working on my master's, I read too much and am haunted by lines that I do not understand. In Dante's *Divine Comedy*, Dante has been guided by his idol, the Roman poet Virgil, through Hell and Purgatory and is about to enter Paradise. Virgil leaves him, saying, "Take henceforth *your* pleasure as your guide." Over the course of his journey, Dante has acquired the wisdom to know where true happiness lies, and will be guided there by his unerring heart. I don't want this to confuse me, but it does.

When I have read too much literature, I go to the gym where I read year-old magazines and run in place on the elliptical machine. Yesterday I read that in a study done on people's happiness, the daily change that had the most impact was taking fifteen seconds each morning to make the bed.

Happiness was easy to find when I came here as a young girl: It was in the quick motion of a goose's neck snatching Wonder Bread from my outstretched hand, or the sound of the lake beneath me the first time I stood on wide, wooden water skis outside Emerald Bay. It was sharp and almost painful, like the jagged summit of a mountain.

Last night, as we sat drinking instant apple cider spiked with vanilla liqueur, I tucked my feet into the warm crease of my boyfriend's knees and told him I was writing about Lake Tahoe. He

tahoe blues

said, "It's like the Fertile Crescent—there's everything here." He meant snow and rivers and the beach and the lake, and afterwards seemed mildly embarrassed to have said it. Later, we made love under the sheets of the bed I'd made that morning, and I realized that the ingredients of my everything are growing smaller now, and I'm learning to be grateful as much for what isn't as for what is. Somehow, the happiness isn't diminished; it's just a little quieter.

My walks with Ruby are becoming a routine. We raise our noses and sniff the air together, crunching through the snow. Some days she is impatient, and will not stay by my side. I try not to mind—she's old, and after all, who knows what's on the to-do list of a dog—but when I walk up the hill from the meadow and see her sprawled across the porch, panting softly, I realize: she's been here all along.

Growing Up in the Tahoe 'Hood
Tim Hauserman

In the 1960s and '70s, I spent my formative years in a neighborhood a few miles outside of Tahoe City. There were a ton of kids to play with just down the street. This was a good thing because we didn't have much in the way of structured programs like soccer/ballet/camp/after-school-whatever, and the last thing our parents would do was drive us to visit other kids.

"What's wrong with the kids down the street?"

In the summer we played Wiffle ball in the neighbor's diamond-shaped driveway. The lamppost was first base, a rock at the top of the driveway second, and the tricky one, a culvert, was third. When we got bored, we would push everybody off the pier into the lake—or at least everybody we knew. This was before all those pesky rules about diving and running on piers and stuff.

Halloween was as Halloween should be. Scary. There were no "it" neighborhoods where parents would bring their kids to a Disney-like extravaganza. It was just wandering around your dark neighborhood until late at night while the parents stayed home. The goal was to accumulate as much candy as possible, and since there were fewer houses we got a good workout.

Speaking of walking, we really did walk a mile up to the school bus and a mile back down, which was OK since we didn't have much homework and only the chores that we never got around to awaited us at home. Fortunately, my mom was nice enough to yell loudly, "I'm home!" as she walked through the front door. We would jump up and say, "Quick, turn the TV off, shovel the deck, stack the firewood, and make your damn bed."

In the fall and winter it was time for touch football on the street. The telephone poles served as the end zones and the edge of the road as the sidelines. You could play with as little as four players. Often I was the youngest, so they would put me with the fastest, whose instructions were simple: "I will hike it and run. As soon as you get the ball, throw it as far as you can."

In the winter we played basketball with a hanger stuffed into the doorjamb as basket and a sock as the ball. Occasionally a parent would show up trying to figure out what all the ruckus was about, but in general the parental philosophy was geared toward avoidance. Just keep it down and be home for dinner.

A few years ago, I took a stroll on my old street and hardly recognized the place. The pier is imprisoned behind a high fence that requires an electronic card to open. The sidelines of our football field are now paved parking spots for manicured tennis courts. The vacant lots that we played on are now fancy second homes. Most startling, the kids are all gone.

Hundred Feet High
Ryan Row

He grunted as he twisted at the waist and threw a shovel-full of snow high and off to the side of our driveway. The sound struck me as wrong, as if I'd just seen a hawk bark, and it stopped me. I glanced off to where he'd thrown the snow. The berms were seven-feet high at least. As high as I could remember ever seeing them. They were like huge wax sculptures of falling ocean waves, and they would melt like wax on the next hot day. I was born in Tahoe, and I'd shoveled the driveway with my dad every season since I could walk. I was fourteen.

I shoveled on a bit more with my head down and my neck exposed to the falling snow. It was snowing hard. A million snowflakes. A billion. More. A number I didn't know. Maybe even a number that didn't exist. That kind of thing was easy to think about. And the snow turned to ice water on my neck. I reached a rectangular patch that was lower than the rest. A car had been there recently. I heard him grunt again. I could almost hear his spine contorting and his stomach and shoulder muscles contracting.

He wasn't five feet away, but I could barely see him—it was snowing that hard. He was dressed all in black, and he looked like a charcoal sketch in progress or a figure that had been burned to a place where no color existed. The berms were higher now. Two or three feet more at least. And he was bent over his shovel like a gravedigger in a war.

"Are you okay?" I asked.

He didn't answer, but he turned back to me. And he may have smiled, but I don't know. I couldn't see his face. He turned away.

"Remember summer?" he said, and I laughed a little at his joke.

It was a joke we made often during long winters.

tahoe blues

A sound like a bag full of heavy chains being dragged came through the storm from the edge of the driveway. I turned just in time to see the huge, industrial yellow plow berming us in. And the other berms were even higher, twenty feet if they were there at all.

"Remember the sun?" I yelled to him.

Again, he didn't answer and just began chipping away at the wall of ice that led to the street. I stared up at the shifting white ceiling of cloud and white dust. And past that ceiling? Who knew. And what would I eat for lunch tomorrow? And who would wake me up for school?

"She'll come back."

"What?" I called to him, through the wall of falling snow.

"She'll come back," he said, a little louder.

"Oh."

I shoveled on and tried my hardest to throw the snow over the berm, but it was too high. So we just kept trying.

A PRAYER FOR TENACITY
Karen Terrey

Desolation Wilderness

Gaze, spent, from that wooden bridge into sheer runnings forked by roots of white bone. The trail hasn't been cleared of last season's deadfall in this forgotten place with winter winds no one measures. The forest is tense with granite muscled by cedar; the lake, a blue horizon. At the flooding, you go right. Each steep switchback measures the length of a line, a breath.

Stop only once against a logged stump to peel an orange. Thick skin drops easily from the globe, a mosaic of juice beading bright as moss, weighty as a fist. Among ancients, you can only be persistent. Rich in rotting detritus, a creek's black surface gleams when late sun shines oblique; pray to make of your own losses such a fertility. A white-haired woman in pink hiking shorts picks her footing down the unkempt trail, clicking her walking pole against scrambling stones. Passing you in a narrows, she grins, *It's strenuous, isn't it?*

Sunrise spills over a crest of the Sierra Nevada. Shivering in the fall chill—can that be the scent of snow in the air?—I name the trees as I pass through the woods: alder, aspen, incense cedar, lodgepole pine, ponderosa. And yellow willow, restless in the wind.

Notebook in hand, I sketch hairy woodpeckers, Indian paintbrush, skyrocket, snakewood.

An ominous crash—through the trees I see a black bear loping toward the water. Blood pounds in my ears.

Then silence, till a squirrel skitters down a cedar, scattering flecks of bark that drift to the forest floor.

Later, at Tahoe's immense blue heart, formed after Mount Pluto erupted twenty-five million years ago, I dip my hand in glacial water. Centuries trickle through my fingers.

IV

turquoise

TACHE DAO
Kai White

For Misti, who swam in the lake and took me out into Tahoe's deep blue water.

From the small sandy cove, the rocks beckoned like humble giants, offering their backs for our feet and hands. My best friend Misti and I frequented this beach on summer breaks from Wooster High School in Reno. On this day the summer sun took a high arch above the lake and the wind stood still. At midday, Misti, sunburned and hot, scrambled across the lower boulders and out onto a high, smooth rock suspended above the water. With a gleam in her eye, she looked back briefly to make sure I was watching and then dove into the lake.

After my usual hesitation, I followed her into that crystal clarity, an aquamarine color—Tahoe before the algae of two-cycle engine pollution. Once we were immersed in the lake, the landscape and the water surrounding us took on a surreal, enchanted quality. Misti kept swimming out farther from the shore, calling for me, and I followed. The shadows of the solid obelisks, flecked with obsidian, stretched across the sand below. The sun streamed around them, down into the deep water, illuminating our bodies, two girls, fifteen and sixteen, swimming through sun and light, our shadows framed in the white sandy lake bottom.

Misti, a WHS swimmer, challenged me to keep up and hid behind a boulder, then popped up out of the water, startling me into a smile. That heart-breaking blue of the water, the white of the lake sand, and the sun catching it all struck a chord in my being that resonates today. Like a geode, compressed until it forms a crystal treasure at its center, the lake shined that day. The boulders held flashes of mica, the gneiss and schist from the glacial thaw that

tahoe blues

carved the alpine lake, castoffs from an ancient epoch. Misti was the rock broken open, a spirit soaring off boulders, a being held and folded into the lake's embrace.

Some girls are inseparable from the waters in which they swim. The summer of 1989 contained a kind of freedom that only a place like Lake Tahoe can hold. There is a wholeness to my memory of Misti and our day in the water of Lake Tahoe—a moment of freedom and openness that will stay with me forever. The lake sustained us, the lake supported us, and the lake was our refuge. Misti, I hope wherever your soul rests, it is a place where your spirit can still soar off boulders into alpine lakes shimmering with sun.

Seeing Blue
Mojie Crigler

At six thousand feet above sea level, where Highway 50 rounds a bend and first sights Lake Tahoe, the road is a ledge, with a mountain to one side and a thousand-foot drop to the other. Only a steel guardrail lines the road.

From Sacramento to Tahoe, Highway 50 climbs, sometimes through towns like Strawberry and Echo, sometimes alongside a river, sometimes out among mountaintops. Whether it's Friday afternoon or Sunday evening or July 3rd or the brats in the backseat fart liverwurst or the dog drools on your ear or the wife is silent and furious or the slowpoke in front or the tailgater in the rear or you need to piss like a motherfucker, or not—coming around that bend and seeing blue Tahoe so big she is elementary, you remember something important and forget something menial. You drink that picture with your nose, for the air up there is clean, clear, sandy, old, boney, rocks, sunshine, lakes formed by meteors so deep you will have vertigo swimming across, shale, donkey ears, Indian paintbrushes, clouds, snow, sticky orange-smelling sap of pine trees—

Pay attention! You almost missed that turn. Your stomach lurched, you yanked the wheel, you thought: My God, what if? You thought: I'll look at the lake later.

In 1958, teenagers Tom Tempest and Beth Sweeney were driving home from their families' remote lakeside cabins where men who had served in the war shaved on back porches using white basins and children spent their days in the water. At night, wood-burning stoves heated the cabins, but if you stepped outside for a smoke or a kiss, you would see in the sky all the stars that existed in the universe and your head would expand in the altitude and so much dark, wild space.

tahoe blues

It was for an experience like this that one old couple approached Lake Tahoe, rounded the curve, and took in the view.

"Wow," he said.

"Gosh," she whispered.

He tapped the brake. Steady, careful. But the distracted driver behind them didn't see the old man slow down. Boom. The old couple's car went through the guardrail and over the cliff.

Beth and Tom approached from the opposite direction. They saw the old couple grasp the sides of the car's interior, mouths moving, faces turning to each other, to outside, calibrating the rapidly changing perspective, realizing the irreversible error, descending into helpless panic as they tumbled over. Beth and Tom heard the woman's brief scream—and then the car was gone. Neither Tom nor Beth said a word. But by the time they arrived at Beth's house in Carmichael, they were laughing so hard it hurt, so hard it made them moan, so hard it felt good.

Firemen had a challenge extricating the couple. They were tied up in each other's arms and legs like twins in the womb, twisted and wrong, as if they'd fallen into a kaleidoscope.

What did they last see?

Sky, rocks, trees, water, Beth, Tom.

THE HOUSE ON TYNER
Dana Arlien

I remember when my dad e-mailed me Ruth's suicide note. Having recently graduated from medical school, I was sitting in the doctor's lounge at Reno's Renown Medical Center. As a psychiatric resident, I was responsible for preventing suicide. Ruth's suicide note felt like a lie.

The first time I saw the house on Tyner Street, I was wearing my newest pair of jeans and soft lavender sweater, thick makeup, and ozone-killing hairspray like adolescent girls wear. My family and I made the long drive up the mountain to Incline Village, circling upwards into the trees until reaching a majestic house. Gene, my father's boss and family friend, opened the door and welcomed us in. The house soared into the trees, spiraling around a central staircase to capture the grandeur of Lake Tahoe. My sister and I were given free range to explore the house. I climbed up and down the stairs, marveling at the different ways the light reflected on the water. I examined African masks from Ruth's sabbatical to the Dark Continent resting on bookshelves and stone bears from Alaska, photos of Europe, and kachina dolls from the American Southwest. I wanted to be her.

In the fall of 1998, I repeated the trek to the house on Tyner to ask Gene for a letter of recommendation for medical school. The house remained stoic and beautiful, light filtering in through the Tahoe pines and playing with patterns on the elegant dining table where I sat with Gene. Ruth was engrossed in her transition from activist for women's rights to author to artist. The room that once was a child's playroom, for their grandchildren, was now a workspace devoted to artistic expression.

tahoe blues

Ruth wrote she had no particular reason to die at this time. She wrote she was not depressed and not in pain. She simply wanted to go on her own terms. She wanted to be in control. I felt her suicide was a hollow and meaningless way to end the life of an educated, elegant woman, a champion for a woman's right to choose, and my role model. I questioned the selfishness of a woman who once fought for others, but in the final moments of her life forgot the impact her suicide could have on her three sons, her grandchildren, and me.

I was sitting in my own living room in Incline Village when my dad called to tell me that Gene had died. Gene, in his eighties, had become confused, and likely had a stroke.

I wanted to see the house again. Unable to remember the name of the street, I drove in circles until I recognized the house where Gene and Ruth once lived on Tyner Street. The house that once held so much magic for me looked sad and neglected. It disappointed me.

THIS LITTLE LIGHT OF MINE
Brandon Pina

"Get the hell off my lap, you lazy broad." Marvin frowned down at the calico piled in his lap and clanked the ice in his tumbler. The hair on the cat's back flicked and shivered. A narrow paw reached out from beneath the mass of fur, claws kneading through Marvin's trousers.

Marvin brushed the cat from its perch and stood up, bent as the feline's tail. Hibiscus was used to the welcoming embrace of Marvin's wife, and now that she'd passed just the two of them shared the empty space. Hibiscus stood with her haunches barely touching Marvin's leg, tail swishing a languid rhythm. "You think you're the queen of the castle now, huh? Well, I'm going out to enjoy the sunset, your highness." Hibiscus slinked around the corner and out of the room.

Marvin opened the door. Taking two gulps, he drank the last trickle of booze and set the glass down on the arm of a chair, sighing when no one nagged him for it. Marvin stared out at the burnt matchsticks the fire had made of the pine trees on Angora ridge. His lone cabin remained, unscathed. He brushed the sparse, stiff hairs on his face with his palm. Grunting in disgust, he burped whisky acid, burning his throat.

"We haven't had any sunlight in the house all day," Marvin said. He began humming a tune he'd sing with his wife as they shoveled snow on sunless days, "This little light of mine, I'm gonna let it shine…" Scanning the yard, Marvin smiled when he found a patch of light glistening off the undulating ice. Marvin put one loafered foot onto the stoop, then another, bracing himself against the door jam. The slick driveway offered no stability, and worse, he felt nothing but the alcohol's warmth and numbness in his feet. Water dripped from icicles and peppered his shoulders. He remembered how she'd fuss over the cold drops that gathered on his collar and stepped wide to avoid them. Then he heard the familiar screech of metal against glass.

"Hibiscus, goddamnit! How many times do I have to tell ya?" Marvin twisted half his body to shoo the cat away. "Get the hell off the blinds." Hibiscus's head arced with Marvin's flailing arm as the old man slipped, his body yielding its rigidity after slamming down into a shallow depression in the ice. Unable to move without feeling the torque of grinding bone in his hip, he turned his face toward the familiarity of his home. He thought he heard his wife's worried tone in a distant coyote's howl. The cold crept over Marvin's body except where the sun warmed him while on its slow decline. He stared, weeping, at the cat in the window who sat looking back at Marvin and the decimated woods.

From a Hiker's Diary
Paul Sohar

Take the steepest trail if you want to be sure of getting there. A downhill trail can only take you back to the car; when hawks are flying closer to the ground, spring must be tickling the wind.

Do not step on a smooth rock when it's wet, even if it lies level with the ground; the other side of the sun shines even brighter and grows bigger boulders.

Do not set a foot between two rocks; even barns take a bow before they collapse.

Do not step on a root that looks like a snake; the broken arms of the oak hold the tatters of summer, and I wear her painted tears in my pocket, balled into a tissue.

Don't believe your legs. They're not in real pain until they crumple under you and start telling stories about you to the rocks; the defrocked cardinal is looking for fig leaves behind the altar. His pudgy hands fall short of his pudenda.

Keep walking until you hear the snow crunch under your feet or the loam give out a low moan now and then. Listen to them, but keep going; even the deer take the marked trail sometimes.

What's this? The Paris metro system? Brooklyn? The copper-mine trail you never found? Forget the maps; getting lost is the ultimate destination, life's promise and fulfillment. When you're lost, you're there and you know it.

Keep on walking. Let the zealots munch on their slogans. Humans too are part of nature, no less, no more; you too have the right to tread the trail as much as the deer or gypsy moths or lightning bolts. Or the last rays of the sun.

The end is now: campfires are lit toward west, the air in your throat demands to rest. If you can't cease to wax poetic even when

tahoe blues

out of breath, remember there is another peak right after death, or at least another cliff that hugs the sky.

Any water tastes better than what drips from your brow, unless it's rainwater. Or snow; loneliness has a statue in a richly decorated room down in the valley, but its doors are always locked. If you knock twice on the white enameled panels, a few notes from a piano will call you in.

Give up? It's too late. Being on the trail, you've given up already; now you have to face what remains. Your boots. Your gloves. The snow that looks so deceptively familiar. More so than the tracks you made only an hour earlier.

The hike is not over when there's nowhere to go and you can't go farther. You can always go further, but you don't have to. There's no end to the hike; it's only that at one point you have to turn around. But don't let anyone but the mountain tell you where and when.

One more thing though: on the way up you're free to follow the call of the sky, but on the way back you must follow the trails. You cannot get lost again. On the way down you have to guard what you found up there.

V

cobalt

KEEP TAHOE BLUE
Joan Atkinson

"I think this is an excellent solution to our problem with water-quality degradation," said Dick, the head of Save Our Lake. He looked at the people gathered around the conference room table. "I have been assured that all further clarity decay will be stopped with just the one treatment."

"We've been looking for something like this," said Bonnie, the woman sitting next to him. Her white cardigan looked like a lab coat. "It's really amazing how research and development in this field have finally reached this pivotal juncture and that we have the opportunity to avail ourselves of the procedure. I think that the results will be incredible. While it's never been done on this scale before, the company assures me we'll be very happy with the results."

"As long as the lake stays as clear and blue as it is right now, I'm all in favor." Stanley ran a hand through his silver hair. "I have rental properties all around the Basin and the primary reason visitors come here is to see a blue Lake Tahoe. If that is compromised at all, I stand to lose a lot of money."

"Is this the only solution?" said Bob, a bearded man in jeans and flip-flops. "It's an extreme and an unnatural attempt to stop a natural progression. What will the public think?"

With a wave of his hand, Dick dismissed Bob's argument. "The public refuses to recognize the sacrifices that have to be made. We, the members of S.O.L., know better and agree that other solutions will not work quickly enough. This is a progressive move toward keeping Tahoe blue for the foreseeable future. After all, we don't want it to become a meadow."

The rest of the group visibly shuddered.

"My main concern is the cost," said Patricia, pulling her suit jacket tighter around her like she was cold. "It seems a little high. As a business owner, I want to make sure I'm getting good value for my contribution to this project."

"The company bidding to do the procedure is willing to absorb any cost overruns. The long-term economical benefits will return the initial outlay one-hundred fold and, of course, the treatment is guaranteed to last quite a long time." Dick shuffled papers together and stacked them neatly in front of him. "Now, are we ready?"

"No," said Bob, glancing around, looking for support. "Let's discuss this some more."

"We're done talking," said Dick, jabbing the table with his finger.

"Let's sign the contract," said Stanley.

"Pay the money," said Patricia.

"And proceed with treatment," said Bonnie.

Dick looked around the table. "It's time to vote. Remember, we've got to approve this by a majority. All those in favor of the motion before this board, raise your hand."

Hands went up around the room, and Dick silently counted them.

"Opposed?"

Bob raised his hand with a resigned look on his face.

"Very well. The motion has passed. Congratulations! We're going to shellac the lake."

Lake Lake
Amy A. Whitcomb

For the seven years I've been living in the foothills of California, Tahoe has been The Most Alluring Place I Intentionally Avoid. It's not that I'm indifferent to the renowned alpine lake; it's that I'm ambivalent toward engaging with its surrounds. Once, while driving from Sacramento to Reno around the southern shoreline, I stopped at Vikingsholm but didn't want to pay for a tour, so I went to Eagle Falls trail but didn't want to herd with the hikers, so I ended up at Harrah's where I made noodles in a camping stove on my tailgate and spilled most of them on the manicured lawn by mistake.

I don't know how to be around Tahoe. When I approach the area, either I want to explore everything or I want to leave it all as is. I can seek or I can find. Am I pillager or pilgrim? The very name for the lake suffered its own identity crisis in the late 1800s. It went back and forth for more than seventy-five years, between Lake Bigler, taken from the then-governor of California, and Lake Tahoe, from the Washoe tribal language. *Tahoe* means big water, high water, water in high place, and, by one interpretation, simply lake.

There's something eerie about the name Lake Lake, the echo, its absurdity. As if accentuating the brimming basin is necessary. And yet, around the edge we've built parking lots and resort properties, a trail from which to look down upon the clear water. What kind of reflection do we want to see?

If I visit Tahoe, a promise of pristine is broken. When a place becomes an icon, we know what to do: pave, partition, privatize—commodify the experience, claim it, Keep Tahoe *Mine*. If I visit Tahoe, I am implicated in this peopling. The grit that pricks my boot soles and rolls, sort of, on its sharp sides as I step adds to erosion. Earthly processes accelerated, or diverted, or truncated, by anthropogenic impact. By pillager and pilgrim and local alike. By mistake, even.

But the promise of pristine is really just a premise; all that Tahoe can be is itself. And what do we do with that? Make bumper stickers that say Keep Tahoe *Tahoe*? Is this an echo that refuses to attenuate—the lake's assertion that it shouldn't always be easy to enjoy? This is what I like about Tahoe: the external and internal ebb and flow, lapping at the bases of high ground. The challenge of a visit is to be appreciative, not appropriative. Isn't that what the cartographers of yore were going for, or did they just need to fill a blank?

And if I don't visit Tahoe, I won't miss much. After all, I can't drive around the lake's edge, windows up, sunglasses on, radio blaring Allman Brothers, without seeing behind the buildings something deep and wide and blue. Lake Lake—how silly the name sounds, how pleasing the idea everlasting is.

IF THE UNSUITABLE NEIGHBOR SMELLS SNOW
Stefanie Freele

Sometimes I think when the neighbors say again, *We're planning for a little snow trip*, I want to trip them with their shiny, matching poles. I don't want to steal their money so I too can go; I just don't want them to ski. Okay, I do want them to go. I mean, someone should enjoy the powder even if we can't because we haven't paid our electric bill. It will be turned off in a week while the nights are window-cracking cold.

It's night skiing I'm talking about. When I zip zip down the tunnel of darkened trees, knowing the chateau is below, but maybe not, maybe it forgot to stay there, because it is so dark-sinister that the lodge at the bottom of the lift might have left.

Back in the school bus days of youth, floors slushy, wool wafts, crumbs of orange crackers on scarves, someone had a sticker that said *don't eat peanut butter, your ski will stick to the roof of your mouth.* I didn't eat peanut butter then on the foggy bus, but instead sat in the back squinting, refusing to wear glasses, keeping my hat on to cover flaccid hair, wishing I was still on the hill, careening through night trees, the ones who reach but can't grasp because I'm so fast.

The entryway to the night forest is the blood-sister to that moment when a diver leaves the blocks and soars dry-suited prior to immersion. Just before the tree line is that gulp-grip in my knees: *maybe the pines won't spit me out at the other end.*

You do that and have a blissful time, I say to Mr. and Mrs. Perky, the neighbors who don't have kids, who have matching Toyotas, bobbed haircuts, silver ski jackets. They glimmer *Toodles!* and skip

tahoe blues

off to their 4WD rig reserved for Tahoe trips. I say by the mailbox in my pajama pants as I drop the overdue water bill, *You guys going to make it for night skiing?*

Not in years! they say, as if I've suggested skipping to San Francisco in their silver jackets. *Oh no, we can't see that well*, as if their four eyes are a collective-vision effort.

Not in years? They are in their fifties. I want to say, *You mean in just a few years I too won't be able to see to ski at night?*

Instead, I stand at the mailbox pretending to shuffle yellow and pink notices.

We're going, I tell my husband when he comes home sweaty, charred, beaten. *Tahoe.*

How? is his only worn-out word.

Apparently on the way in, he didn't notice our missing and unused bikes, sold on Craigslist this afternoon.

When he sleeps, I siphon-spit gas from the neighbor's Toyota tanks: fill ours for the way there, fill a can for the way back.

I have a spare key of theirs to feed the cats. I'm trustworthy that way. I empty a third of their almonds, sneak four slices of bread, two tuna cans out of twelve, a bagful of tangerines off their tree.

Ready? I say to my husband who has fallen asleep on the couch. I've packed everything. All he has to do is sit in the car and let me take him for a ride.

Two Drops
Dave Murcar

I do not understand. You want to leave so badly, and I simply don't get it. Why? What's wrong with this place?

Because I just have to. This place is not for me. I don't fit here. I want to be where the action is. I want to be *Big Time!* I want to be a part of Lake Tahoe! That's where things happen, not this backwater.

Nobody wants to be that lake. It's dirty. It's huge. You don't know where all those drops have been.

You're afraid. You live your life in this place, and I know Fallen Leaf Lake is as beautiful as it gets. All the water is pure and clean. Every drop is perfect. Everyone is the same. They think the same. But that is the very thing that makes me feel stifled. I can't be myself. There is more to the world. In Tahoe you can come across anything. There could be salt. There could be silt.

There could be motor oil.

There could be motor oil. But I'm willing to take that chance. That's the price of living life on your own terms. I can't live my life in the community comfort zone. I feel as if my very soul is telling me that I need to get out to stay alive.

I still don't see what's wrong with this place.

There is nothing wrong with this place. It's idyllic. It's fabulous. Every water drop probably wishes they were here. So, everyone is convinced there must be something wrong with me, but I'm just made for a different place. And if I stay here... I'm sure everyone in Tahoe wishes they were part of Fallen Leaf. But I just need something different.

I wish you didn't have to go.

I'm sorry I called this place a backwater. I feel like I'm losing my mind.

Any idea of how you'll get there?

Not really. I was so desperate a few weeks ago that I thought maybe I could evaporate from the surface.

How do you know you'd come down on Tahoe?

I don't at all. I could land anywhere. It was a stupid idea. I stayed away from the surface, obviously. I'm desperate but I'm not crazy yet.

I think I might have an idea for you. I heard there is a spillway on the north end. There is some kind of barrier you have to work your way around, but if you can get to it I heard the spillway dumps you into some insane ride that ends up in Tahoe.

For real?!

Yeah.

Oh my God, thank you. Thank you!

When you enter Tahoe you'll be entering with a bunch of other newbies. Maybe you'll make some friends on the ride and you won't have to be alone when you get there.

Wow, that would be great.

I'm going to miss you.

I know. I wouldn't go if I didn't have to. I'm going to miss you too.

Angora Monster
Shawn Huestis

Upon the twenty-fourth day of June, in the year 2007, terror struck the town of South Lake Tahoe. Scars from the monster's rampage still lie like shadows across the woodland, for it was deep within this forest that the nightmare had birthed.

The beast was condemned to starve until death. Though, a hasty guard left it faintly breathing. Even weak, the wretch shivered with cleverness. It crept from its circular cage of stones. Wind threatened the very life of it. The creature endured by nibbling arid foliage. Yet no matter how much it ate, a curse filled the horror with eternal hunger.

Mouths split open all across its restless form. From them, tongues danced madly amidst rings of snapping fangs. The combined roar deafened without any breath of ending. Growing larger, the beast stalked trees forbidden from fleeing. All their dry arms could not fend it off. The leviathan devoured them and everything else in its horrid wander.

Thousands of dwellings stood defenseless against its approach. Though these particular trees had been carved and painted into quaint houses, the hellion still craved them. Townsfolk rushed whilst terror shoved at their backs into packing only their most treasured possessions lest they be devoured in their dwellings. Gnawing hundreds of homes down to their masonry, it roared cruelly at the tragedy trailing it.

With hundreds of townsfolk fleeing, only the Knights in Red Helmets dared charge in. Two thousand strong risked the quest of slaying the nightmare. They took bravery from knowing its weakness. That it had no thirst. Armed with cannons firing spears of water, they besieged it.

The behemoth roared in fury whilst expelling its blackened toxin. Lighter than feathers, the winds swiftly carried this vile shadow over the entire woodland. Poison stung even the lungs of townsfolk from neighboring lands. The knights only survived the monster's venom and countless talons as it all fell upon their woven armor. They cast down lines of ruby powder, which forbade the creature from crossing.

Nimble despite all its immensity, the horror swiftly clawed up the trees. It lunged from crown to crown over the lines of crimson potion, crushing down upon the knights who shielded themselves beneath silver blankets. Desperate, the knights grasped their axes and swung into trees still standing before the leviathan's path. Unable to leap across the toppled crowns, the beast fell into the knights' trap.

The monster thrashed for days whilst impaled by spikes of water. It snapped and clawed at the Knights in Red Helmets. Yet, they pressed ever closer around the withering creature. It frantically tried hiding in the dark skeletons it left. Though, with no further wood to feast on, it at last starved to death.

The vile shadow vanished from the land. Townsfolk rejoiced for the horror's slaying. Since that dark time, new dwellings have risen from the rubble. Though, the monster's victims still wonder if during some arid summer, another careless act might resurrect it...

A Summer Without Blue
Eve Quesnel

My neighbor says, "It's like Armageddon." I'm thinking the movie; he's thinking the Bible. However we look at it, it seems like the world is ending.

Summer of 2008, dry lightning storms ignite two thousand fires in California, much too early in the season, and illuminate the state with orange fireworks, then cover it with powdery ash. In our small Sierra mountain town, Truckee, we escape such ignitions. Nevertheless, a gray film infuses our region. For days, I yearn to rise up and out of the choking air, but charcoal-shaded mornings drift slowly like fog, sink into gunmetal afternoons, and smother evening's dusk with a heavy gray cloak. From a blazing world beyond, a silent smoke-infused beast has crept into the mountains and with one expended breath made all objects disappear.

Visitors from around the world anticipate the majestic scenery of the snow-peaked crown that surrounds Lake Tahoe, and the bluest of blue water that brings them to the largest alpine lake in North America, named the "jewel of the Sierra" by Mark Twain. But this summer, the Caribbean turquoise that outlines the perimeter of the lake, revealing car-size boulders before transitioning to a darker cobalt blue, succumbs to haze. The only view the tourists will see is gray sky hovering above a circular bowl. Those who have made the trek to Tahoe will return home without memorable photographs of the famous lake, their stories only able to recount adventures in smoky mountains. "The health of the eye," Emerson said, "seems to demand a horizon. We are never tired, so long as we can see far enough." But we can't see far enough, we can't even distinguish light from dark, shade, shadow, shapes of any kind. In my house, I see all objects, but outside… outside is simply an idea.

In February 2009, state water officials call on Californians to reduce water use by 20 percent, "to ease a drought that could be the next serious hit to California's economy." They also suggest we change our way of thinking and consider water a precious commodity. The color of Lake Tahoe and its blue ceiling is also a prized gift. How can we keep fires at bay, and the mountain air and grand natural lake clear and blue?

Near my home, Brockway Summit offers a 360-degree view of Lake Tahoe. To reach the crest, my tired Subaru climbs, once again, to make the short trip over the mountain. When I arrive at the high point that overlooks the lake, I gasp. I always do. Blue, pulled from above, fills the lake, and the sun's white stars glimmering on its surface paint the quintessential alpine scene. After experiencing the claustrophobic summer of 2008, I now relish in the color that has made Lake Tahoe and its brilliant ceiling famous. Blue sky, blue Lake Tahoe, may just be the most beautiful thing, a marvel of nature, the essence of purity.

A NARROW MARGIN OF COLOR
Jeanine Stevens

South Lake Tahoe, January 1, 2010

It's autumn, time for the kokanee to spawn. Walking up Taylor Creek from the lake, we follow the flash of carnelian in clear water. They struggle in shallows, the small heart spinning, the red gills heaving. The entire body is flushed with red, the head reptilian and olive green. We learn the hooked jaw is useful in mating, a part of sexual selection for females. The stream is choked with color as they complete their life cycle in a blaze of fire. You take a photo that resembles a banner of velvet ribbons, and I remember the Celtic saying, "A woman who wears a salmon tattoo on her ankle can travel anywhere." On December 31, we stay up past midnight to see the blue moon. In white star-scented air, it is surrounded by a large ring: translucent, ocular fuzz, a barely-there-blue. A glacial spectrum, I think moongarten, and know night holds this landscape. Next day, we snowshoe in the meadow, the sun so bright; we make a quick stop to rest our eyes. There in deep shade, a neon blue that disappears in bright sun. You say, "It's the water content that makes crystals seem electrified, a filament lit from within." We stomp around trees, in and out of light, testing our perception—such a narrow margin of color absorbed. I've seen the sign above small taverns, a martini glass with an olive, just-that-blue, and on paint chips: *Feather Falls*, *June Lake*, and *Carthage*, but the closest I come is Chagall's pencil writing the sky over Vitebsk.

VI

ultramarine

PROLOGUE
David Higginbotham

Drive east on I-80. Three hours from San Francisco. Cross the valley and climb the green wall of the Sierra. At this altitude, the population density thins. It is as if people, pulled by gravity, have all collected at the edge of the Pacific.

Off the exit into Truckee stands a statue of a pioneer. Fitting. Donner Pass is memorial to what we will do to survive. This cracked blacktop, often impassible in winter, rolls along contour lines and erodes into landscape. Here in the thin blue haze of a High Sierra dawn, blowing snow drifts across glacial lakes lost in Tahoe's shadow. They may as well not exist.

They are easily forgotten. And they would be. Except one. A few feet from shore, what remains of a cowboy boot interrupts the frozen surface. You would have had to see it before now to know it was a boot. It is indistinguishable, partially embedded in the ice. The scavengers have torn through the red wool sock beneath. The skin around the pad of the foot is gone. Two toes are missing. The others are a mess of gnawed tissue and fragments of frozen bone. Coyotes have chewed off the sole. I have interrupted them at their work. Their tracks are the only marks in the new-fallen snow. And mine.

From shore, the startling red of the frayed sock against what little is left of the cracked leather gives the impression of an icy water garden with a strange and solitary bloom. But it won't stay this way. The Steller's jays tease the threads of yarn for their nests. And the ice will melt.

He is, or was, a Caucasian male, mid-forties—but no one will know until spring. Until then, there is this small comfort: he is still here.

tahoe blues

EIGHT HOURS
Suzanne Roberts

I

At lunch, Brandon ate as many tater tots as he wanted. He ate cake until he felt sick. I couldn't eat.

II

On our way to the lift, my supervisor had pulled me aside. "Brandon's father hit an aspen tree on his first run of the day. His aorta detached. He was dead by the time patrol got there." The family decided to let Brandon finish ski school, enjoy his sixth birthday, before finding out. Before the world changed.

"Let me carry your skis, Brandon." The voice cracking on its own.

"Carry mine."

"Me too."

"And mine."

"It isn't your birthday," said the pit in the throat. "It's only Brandon's birthday."

III

The aspen tree is part of a clonal colony derived from a parent tree. Each clone lives above ground for up to 150 years. The root system can live underground thousands of years. The aspen on the edge of the intermediate run still adds to its rings. New clones emerge from the earth. The man who hit the tree has been gone for fifteen years. Brandon is now twenty-one, and every birthday is the anniversary of his father's death. The aspen tree will be there even after he's gone.

IV

Brandon was the last one to be picked up. We always referred to the stragglers as "the least loved children," their parents drinking hot toddies at the bar. But I didn't even think it. Instead, I let him choose a video, sat with him as he laughed at the animated figures.

V

The bark of an aspen is white and soft and strong.

VI

The mother finally came in with the ski patrol. "Mommy," he called. She hugged him. Her face scrunched up in a red and swollen way. She left without looking at me, without knowing that Brandon learned to hockey stop, that he had moved up to a level five. None of it mattered. Gravity had changed everything.

VII

"I want to ski in front."
"Well, I want a million dollars."

tahoe blues

"But why can't *I* ski in front?"

"You can ski second behind Brandon."

"Why does Brandon get to ski in front the *whole* time?"

"It's his birthday."

"It was my birthday last week. And I want to go through the bear cave first."

"It isn't your birthday today. It's only Brandon's birthday today. Let's sing to him while we ski."

VIII

"You can't cry," my supervisor had said. "You have to make sure that little boy has a good time." Good time, good time, good time. The not-knowing-yet day. Happy birthday, dear Brandon, happy birthday to you. We sing and we ski. We play airplanes and race cars. We play and we play at pretending.

THE DEER SKULL
Kimberly Covill

Back in November we used to sit on our old deck, the deer skull resting on one massive antler in front of us. Skin and fur still clung to the nose. The eyes still shined. You could see the tongue, pink and swollen, through gaps in the teeth.

"You should bury it and have worms decompose it," I said one evening, sipping wine and staring into the eyes. The thing was dead and yet not dead.

"Too cold, ground's already frozen," Luke replied. "I was thinking I could boil it, get all the rotting stuff out … make it into a coat rack or something." I thought about the skull and antlers, shellacked and preserved forever.

By December the fur was gone. Something with little teeth had chewed away some of the nose. It still looked good, though. It was a noble skull, one that lived a fine country life—Luke's prized shot.

When we moved we tied it in the back of his truck with a piece of twine, on top of the snowmobile. I stared at it as I drove behind, the few times I was close enough. Luke drove too fast, and I drove too slow.

At our new house, he grabbed the skull and twine. He held up the underside for me to see the rotting flesh and brains, and where he'd cut across the neck with his buck knife.

"Gross!" I squirmed and turned away at the purple and brown lumps of tissue, the sawed off bone and veins. He laughed and tied it up in the tree by one antler. We stood and marveled. We were probably the only people in Tahoma with a rotting deer skull hanging off a tree outside our front door.

"Looks good, don't it?"

tahoe blues

"There's your little piece of the country," I said. He was always talking about the country, how that's where he should be instead of here in a neighborhood.

One morning there was a dog standing underneath the skull, sniffing up at it and wagging a shaggy tail. Then a few different dogs were taking turns standing up on their hind legs to get closer to it, nosing it and making it sway. When it snowed they could reach it easily, gnawing and licking.

We didn't sit outside much anymore.

One day in March, I came home from work and Luke was gone. The picture of the horses on the wall, his homemade mugs, all gone. My heart sunk to my feet.

I stepped outside to get some air, staring down at the dirty snow path into our house for a long time. So that was it. When I looked up, there was the skull, swaying slightly and hardly recognizable. Half the nose was gone. The tongue had been eaten all the way up to the brain, and the eyes were black holes. I reached up and untied the twine, surprisingly easy, letting the skull fall to the snow. In the morning, it was gone.

THE FOURTH FRIEND
Alison Bender

It wasn't the sudden, sharp breeze that woke Annie, but a feeling of alarm. She listened to Derek's breathing—the soft inhaling and exhaling a welcome reprieve from most of their interactions lately—before opening her eyes to the blackness of her small room. Nothing.

She sighed and turned in her bed, but a light from the window caught her attention and she tiptoed toward it, watching as bands of moonlight leapt mischievously from Lake Tahoe's sparkling waters to the shiny snow of the nearby mountainside.

"Ghosts?" Hazel, the leathered, wiry owner of the Sleeping Bear B and B, had laughed at Derek's question. "No one asks about the ghosts anymore!"

Derek leaned closer while Annie, still upset about their latest fight, pushed her leftover pancakes into a frown on her plate.

"My grandfather, the Sleeping Bear's original owner, died young," Hazel's voice assumed the low undertone of a confidante. "He was skiing with four of his friends when he got lost in the trees. For whatever reason, his friends didn't report him missing until the next day, when it was much too late. He'd broken his leg, but it was the cold that killed him.

"The next time each of his friends went skiing, they died—one ran into a tree, one fell off a lift, and one hit his head on a rock. However," Hazel licked her lips, "the fourth friend never skied again; he died of old age just last year. Some people say that my grandfather won't be satisfied until a fourth person dies."

Annie frowned at her plate. She didn't believe in ghosts—she'd come only because this getaway seemed like the last chance to rekindle a dying romance. Now, as she stood at the window, Hazel's words echoed in her memory. The transient moonlight was the last thing Annie saw as she faded back into sleep.

Derek was gone when Annie awoke in the morning. She found him eating breakfast with Ted and Irene, the other couple staying at the Sleeping Bear, whom he'd skied with the day before and planned to ski with again. Hazel poured her coffee.

"You should come," Irene said. "Yesterday was fun."

"I'm not good," Annie said. "And I don't have gear."

"Nonsense," Hazel chimed in. "You'll borrow mine. We're about the same size."

"You should, Annie," Derek said.

She turned to him, surprised. Yesterday, he couldn't leave her behind quickly enough. "If you want me to come, I will," she said slowly.

It was a long few seconds before, almost shyly, Derek smiled. "Please come." Outside, the sunlight danced from the shimmering waters to the snow-covered slopes.

They bundled into warm clothes, laughing together at their bulky outfits. Derek kissed Annie's cheek as he headed outside. "We'll meet you at the gondola," he said.

A minute later, Hazel came out with a pair of boots, skis, and poles. "You'll have fun," she promised. "And that's very nice of you—they needed a fourth friend."

Into the Blue
Kailyn McCord

He hands her snowshoes and buckles them, crimping industrial strapping onto her feet. They walk to the meadow, which she knows in summer is an estuary, but what they call now in winter a meadow anyway. It is white and clear and ringed with trees, exactly the place to go snowshoeing.

The house—full of his family, cousins, and girlfriends of cousins, air mattresses sprawling across the rooms—falls away behind them. Over the past days they've waded around each other, around the suitcases open in various states of disorganization, around bodies groggy, still sleeping or hungover. Outside, she breathes deep gulps of air.

They trudge, and her shoes lose their initial bind. She hates this about snow sports: the constant adjusting of gear, the always-improper fit, the sure feeling that, although everyone else seems well adjusted, these contraptions have it in for her.

They pause at the top of a ridge, the bank of the estuary buried far beneath the snow, blue-black dirt hibernating. She squints against the whiteness.

"You should take pictures," she says.

"Yeah. I don't know about the lens in this cold."

"It would be great though. We could even get costumes… there's thrift stores in town?"

"Maybe. Nothing's open tomorrow though." He stares ahead.

The impracticality of the idea grows: her dresses back home, her festival dresses, are not here; the cousins would want to stay inside and watch college football games; and even if his camera could take the cold, he'd worry the whole time.

"Wanna head back?" he asks.

"Sure."

But she doesn't. They've been out barely an hour, her body just warming up beneath the layers to make its own heat. She follows him back to the garage. They knock their boots against the stairs with short, hollow sounds.

Two weeks later they will return home, and he will leave her. It will be sudden. He will confess his love for another woman, and it will hit her in the belly, a twisting in the organs. The first night without him, she will dream of the meadow.

She wears one of her dresses in the dream, a blue, iridescent, bejeweled bust, no sleeves, a wide skirt down to the snow. She stands in the middle of the meadow, barefoot. She brushes her hand along shrubs, balances a cocktail glass of pink liquid in the other. She laughs to no one. Black sunglasses like bug eyes cover her face, her mouth full of teeth and the red inside flesh of a mouth. She looks for him, shouts for him, look how well it turned out, look, just look at the color! The blue on the white, the blue on her skin, the white coming up between her toes, quick, take the picture! She smirks, like she knows a secret that he knows too, her lips against the glass, a gaudy show. She looks and looks, and awakes with a sharp breath, eyes open and spinning in the blue.

THOSE DEAD LITTLE FISHES
Mike Pielaet-Strayer

All the fish are dead. I see them there, thousands of dead fish, floating atop the lake's surface in lifeless buoyancy, their bulging white bellies glittering under the sun. Those dead fishes. Belly-up and stinking. The fish are always first. That's the way it went in Michigan, then in Minnesota, then in Utah, and then in Nevada—and everywhere between—and that's the way it will surely go here, in sunny South Lake Tahoe. First the fish. Then the birds. And, lastly, the mammals. That's been the order of extinction since the accident. Fish, birds, mammals. Implacable and unstoppable as the shifting of the seasons.

Not even the minnows escape.

It's been a month since we were told of the accident. One month, since the government made its announcement. *Something's happened,* they said. Our last rites. One month since the virus known as A3N2 was unwittingly loosed on humanity. Our death sentence. *No cure exists…* One month, millions dead.

God help us all…

Birds squawk in the sky above. I watch them. *How long?* I wonder.

The world reacted differently to the news of imminent demise than the government anticipated. Instead of looting, riots, and violence, there was only this kind of hopeless resignation and this coming together—this unification, this mass-spread love. It's strange, how in times of tragedy people flock to one another for support, but in moments of peace we seem hell-bent on destruction.

The sun sinks below the horizon, casting neon shafts of light across the firmament, and the perpetual snow-cross of Mount Tallac incandesces blood red. The jagged folds of the Sierra, radiant and grand in the fiery dusk, are like the crumbling walls of some deity's palace. Glowing, glowing, glowing, in this—the hour of twilight. As

tahoe blues

I stare at the mountains, tears in my eyes, a bird falls from the sky like a banished angel, and somewhere a dog begins to whine. An odd taste comes to my mouth. It coats my throat, and I cough. Another bird lands wooden at my feet.

The sun dips.

A final lash of evanescent light whips the crimson heavens.

Darkness.

QUAKES
June Sylvester Saraceno

The year my marriage fell apart a series of earthquakes were rattling Northern California, all the way up to my quiet mountain town. Most occurred at night. I would wake as the bed trembled and the wine glasses hanging over the kitchen sink violently toasted themselves but didn't shatter. In fact, none of the quakes caused any real damage, but I soon became hyper-quake-sensitive. In fact, I began to feel them every night. I would wake trembling in bed, distinctly feeling the bed, not myself, shaking. Usually I'd scan the news the next day for reports of the epicenter and scale of these quakes. Rarely was there even a mention. I began to realize I must be living on a fault line, or maybe a fault divot, so that the quakes were moving through my house but not necessarily anywhere else. It was unsettling. I became so aware of these movements that even during the day, standing at the checkout register or during my break, if I closed my eyes too long I'd tilt toward that dark vertigo, feeling the shifting plates.

There was no one to tell about this, really. The girls in the drugstore where I work are all in their twenties, single, not at all interested in what goes on in a home or a bed with only one person in it. My husband hasn't contacted me since he left that night and never concerned himself much about the house or property anyway. So, I've begun to keep a detailed record of the quakes: time, duration, and strength as well as I can measure it. It's all I can do. Sometimes I'm up five or six times a night adding to the records. I've rigged a little cap with a light on it, sort of a softer version of a coal miner's apparatus, so I can see the notebook pages without turning on the reading lamp. I keep it on the pillow next to me and the notebook next to it so when I feel the tremors, I can simply reach out and record the measurements. I record the time exactly as it is reflected from the nightstand clock, and for the duration and strength of the quakes I've developed a system of lines and stars. I only use black ink. I think it lasts longer. I've stocked up on pens and notebooks and I intend to keep recording as long as the quakes continue. I believe one day these records will be of use. The weather service or perhaps environmental researchers may find them useful. Perhaps they will be able to explain the peculiar, narrow focus of the quakes.

It Felt Good
Tom Wendell

After the sleepless nights and many hours of sitting, it felt incredibly good, if oddly foreign, to move my body. My arms and legs pumped through their well-rehearsed and synchronized motions, my lungs expanding and contracting and my heart intensifying its unceasing task as I fell into a steady rhythm. The freshly fallen snow beneath my cross-country skis was soft and I moved with surprising speed. I transitioned from a section of fairly dense pine forest to the edge of the burn area with its somber, blackened trees standing sentinel over the now open, gently rolling terrain. Their coal black trunks stood in stark contrast to the pristine, white snow with its glistening, multicolored refractions of the fading sunlight. Nature was providing me with an almost surreal sense of gliding through time. It seemed fitting… not only for the scene that unfolded before me, but for my state of mind. I was taking one of my short, infrequent breaks from the now weeklong vigil of attending to my beloved mother as she slowly succumbed to her inevitable death from renal failure at the age of eighty-nine.

Should I feel guilty that I was not by her side and was instead experiencing the healing effect of endorphin release amidst nature's beauty while she was drawing what might be her last few breaths? In my confused, sleep-deprived condition it was hard to know how to feel. Along with my brother and cousin and the incredible nurses from the hospice program, a close family friend and a steady stream of well-wishers stopped by the house daily. She was virtually never alone and was well looked after. We all needed to take breaks from the emotionally and physically exhausting duty of seeing her through her final process, one that would unfold in its own way in its own time. No, guilt was not an appropriate emotion here. If she were fully conscious, she would heartily approve of my decision to take some time to recharge my emotionally and physically drained batteries. After all, it was she who instilled in me a love of nature and respect for its capacity to heal. It was she who introduced me to the sport of skiing, so I was in some sense an extension of her consciousness, and certainly of her flesh.

It was a transcendent moment for me as I shed the shroud of guilt anxiety, and my mind wandered back to the few words I had exchanged with her the previous evening. In one of her rare moments of semi-lucidity, I was able to lock eyes with her and speak with her in her native German. I told her that she was a remarkable woman and asked her if she understood me. She held my gaze and, with what little strength she had, nodded her head and gently squeezed my hand. A wan smile came across her troubled but still beautiful face. It was a moment I will cherish until the time I draw my own last breath and lose consciousness for eternity.

Varying Depths
Erin Costello

We started it—sure as the rakes saved the neighbors and turned the lake green. Once a tourist asked me how we separated the colors of the lake. I told her about the special pens we used called *varying depths*. She thanked me and said that the contrast was lovely.

I had locked our keys in the car at Echo so we hitched a ride there from Lily Lake. At about 1:45 p.m. we took North Upper Truckee Road back toward our marsh. We wouldn't admit it, but we were thrilled to be in a car and out of our backpacks and expensive performance layers. The smoke followed us like a compliment; our conversation and attention were on a verbal daydream about a cheese-centered lunch. By the time we had eaten lunch, the governor was still a week away from lifting the weight set that didn't burn.

By the same time the next day I was reading pieces of books off the asphalt. I picked up a page out of a children's story that disappeared into a black smear on my fingers. A small section of a screen door was stuck to my windshield, and I left it there as I looked out over the water. The layers were gone but there was a volcano in the reflection, houses and trees popping then ghosts and ash drifting over the rest of us.

Down at the beach a twentysomething man was crying as he safely watched the mountainside burn. He watched the house he had grown up in sizzle and pop. He popped the top of the beer in his hand, and ashes of photographs fell inside.

Breathing was getting difficult. I had already called some friends in Sacramento but was afraid I might not get back into town. The disaster tourists from Nevada, Mammoth, and Bakersfield had arrived, but we were all used to tourists of varying ethical standards.

84

tahoe blues

No one lives in Tahoe, and it doesn't snow in California. I still wish it had been the second homes, the Vail homes that had gone.

A year later, I moved to Colorado. Angora had stopped burning, but the state had ignited. Under the same oppressive, red glowing sky, I watched the valley from the swimming pool of my parent's South Bay hilltop home. Where lightning struck, smoke, then sirens followed. There were no depth tiles in the pool, no color for the deep end, no contrast.

"You built in a forest," someone from Boston said.

You and I looked at each other because we knew we had started it. We were driving home on North Upper Truckee Road at 1:45 p.m. on Sunday, June 24, 2007. We saw the smoke behind us. The news said it started at 2:15 p.m. on Sunday, June 24, 2007, at Seneca Pond. We had never been to Seneca Pond.

"We started it," the young man replied, then finished his beer.

VII

sapphire

BLUE WATERS
Pamela Warman

All of a sudden his smell bothers me; everything bothers me because this cancer is scorching my skin from the inside. I cannot stand odors, my eyes are dilated and sensitive, and light hurts me. And my bones, Grandma, my bones!

I feel like I'm a prisoner in the Tower of London, tied to the rack where my limbs get stretched a little bit more with each turn of the wheel. Slowly but surely, how much this suffering hurts me. Still, I remember the birth of my first son hurting a thousand times more! That pain I was supposed to forget, but thoughts of infanticide remain tattooed on my forehead. This new pain lasts for days varying in intensity like waves entering my brain, my bones, my heart.

I see a tree outside I can change into. I stare at its bark and I become the tree. Since I was very young I've played this game, out of curiosity with nature and animals. Now, when I meditate, I see the similarities with this childhood game.

There is a bird now, perhaps a raptor, with sharp claws digging into my neck, squeezing my throat, making me bleed and never letting go.

In my stomach a desperate rat eats my insides away, carving my death with stubborn determination. I sit up on the couch, and barely opening my eyes I look out the window. It is beautiful Tahoe, the pine trees softly moving with the breeze, squirrels running on the porch. A blue jay squeals, and I cover my ears.

Feeling the need to move, I rise to the occasion. My hips remind me that I'm being poisoned with chemotherapy. I feel a rod of steel going across my hips, stiff, aching, so painful I question if I will ever walk again.

I lean forward to rise, and my ribs remind me that it's not just my hips, but every bone in my body. Pins and needles attack me from every angle. I look for a way out of this reality, but there is no escape and nobody here to help.

I left my husband before the cancer. Now I sit here looking out the window wondering how nice it would be to have a husband to take care of me while I'm sick. Oh fuck it! I have myself to pick up the pieces. Who needs a husband anyway?

I make one more effort and I slide the window open; a little breeze comes in to touch me. Slowly I inhale the smell coming from outside... Jeffreys, ponderosas, cedars, and aspens, all from this mountain paradise.

I am not giving up. I rise again and I can see the lake. Then and there I decide to play again. I become the water. Closing my eyes I leave the forest and the animals behind. I am diving into the lake; in its blue waters I will heal my pain, my disease, and my lonely heart.

Aguas Azules
Pamela Warman

Me molesta de pronto su olor; me molesta todo porque este cáncer me enrosca la piel por dentro. Los olores no los aguanto, los ojos dilatados y sensibles, y la luz me causa tanto dolor. ¡Y los huesos, Abuelita, los huesos!

Me siento que estoy presa en la Torre de Londres, atada a la mesa de torturas en donde cada vuelta mis miembros son estirados cada vez más. Lento pero seguro, cuánto me duele este sufrimiento. Aún así recuerdo el nacimiento de mi primer hijo doliéndome ¡mil veces mas! Ese dolor debía olvidarlo, pero los sentimientos de infanticidio permanecen tatuados en mi frente. Este nuevo dolor dura días y varia en intensidad como olas entrando en mi cerebro, mis huesos, mi corazón.

Puedo observar un árbol afuera en el cual me puedo transformar. Me concentro en su corteza y me convierto en ella. Desde muy temprana edad practiqué este juego, nacido de pura curiosidad hacia la naturaleza y los animales. Ahora, cuando medito, veo la gran similitud con este juego de mi infancia.

Hay un ave ahora por ejemplo, un ave de rapiña similar a una águila pequeña, con garras afiladas incrustadas en mi cuello, apretando mi garganta, haciéndome sangrar sin piedad.

En mi estómago una rata desesperada, comiéndome las entrañas, esculpiendo mi muerte con obstinada determinación. Me siento en el sofá, y apenas abriendo los ojos miro por la ventana hacia fuera. Es el hermoso Tahoe, los pinos moviéndose suavemente con la brisa, las ardillas corriendo por el balcón. Un pájaro azul grita, y me tapo los oídos.

Me levanto a la ocasión que siento de caminar un poco. El primer impacto son las caderas recordándome que estoy siendo envenenada con quimioterapia. Siento una barra de acero atravesando mis caderas, dura, tan doloroso que me pregunto si podré volver a caminar.

Me echo hacia delante para levantarme del sillón, y las costillas me recuerdan que no son solo las caderas sino cada hueso de mi cuerpo. Agujas punzantes atacándome desde cada ángulo; busco un escape de esta realidad, pero no hay salida y nadie aquí para ayudarme.

Dejé a mi pareja antes del cáncer. Ahora sentada aquí mirando por la ventana me pregunto cuán cómodo habría sido tener un marido que cuidara de mí durante esta enfermedad. ¡A la mierda con eso! Me tengo a mí misma para recoger los pedazos del suelo. ¿Quién necesita un marido después de todo?

Hago un esfuerzo más y abro la ventana; una suave brisa se cuela por la rendija y me toca delicadamente. Despacio inhalo el aroma de afuera… Jeffreys, ponderosas, cedros, y aspens, todos árboles de este paraíso montañoso.

No me voy a dar por vencida. Me levanto una vez más y puedo ver el lago. En ese instante decido que quiero volver a jugar. Me convierto en el agua. Cerrando mi ojos abandono el bosque y los animales. Me lanzo en el lago; en sus aguas azules voy a sanar mi dolor, mi enfermedad, y mi solitario corazón.

So Close to Home
Sherry Sellars

When the last teen parent picked up her baby at Mt. Tallac High School nursery, I whipped into action. After cleaning up and turning off the lights, I grabbed my keys, ignored the ringing phone, and slipped out the door. Throwing a quick goodbye to Ginger, my co-teacher, I slid into my car before I heard her reply.

This past week had been the busiest this year. Today we had four babies under a year, two sixteen-month-olds, and three toddlers. The hours flew past as Ginger and I diapered, fed, soothed, and played referee. Now I wanted to go home and drink a lot of wine, something I've avoided the last few months.

Roaring onto Emerald Bay Road, I zipped by a local man on his bike. His bike trailer held an upright sign with the words "Jesus Loves You" slopped on with cheap paint.

"The hell he does," I murmured. Squealing through the "Y" onto Lake Tahoe Boulevard, I zigzagged through traffic, recalling the phone call with my doctor earlier today.

"There was absolutely no sign of ovulation this month. We may want to consider switching from Clomid to… something else." More fertility drugs and stronger doses. How was I going to tell Dave?

I raced to a stop at Grocery Outlet. Twenty minutes later, I shot back out, mouth sore from pretending to smile after running into a chatty friend. Barely making the light at Al Tahoe, I flipped off the driver of the red Subaru who honked.

In six months, I'd be forty-two. Was it time to throw in the towel?

Passing by Sprouts, I debated whether to stop for a Bee Sting smoothie, but I couldn't face another conversation—so, one final stop.

I jogged into the library and picked out a few DVDs. Scurrying back, I flung them on the passenger seat. Whipping out of the parking lot, I almost made the light at Lake Tahoe Boulevard.

"Goddamnit!" My eyes filled as I smacked the steering wheel again and again.

A flash of color caught my attention. Straight ahead, a parasail drifted over Lake Tahoe, a rainbow bubble in a sapphire sky. I followed its path until an osprey flew in view, hovering over the turquoise water near the shore. Wings bent and eyes intent on the water, the osprey suddenly bolted toward the dark-blue center of the lake. That was when I noticed the mountains on the north side—the Watson Range. They sat splendid and silent, as though assembled for a coronation. Summits were sugared with snow, though it was already June. Evergreens, in vivid contrast with the peaks, speckled the lower half of the mountains. Swirling above, cirrus clouds, white and fleecy, danced a slow waltz with a docile breeze.

A sharp honk brought me back. The light was green. Looking into my rearview mirror, I saw that I was smiling. Giving the driver behind me a brief wave, I drove on. So close to home.

BAPTISM
Janice Wilson Stridick

I drove, all night, away from a failed marriage and a chafing family.

My tiny yellow Honda 600, stuffed with my life, took the last leg of desert cool and easy. Just after dawn, I began the ascent to the mile-high lake. As I made it over the top, the blue, blue lake stood up the sky. I parked and got out to stare, to breathe the rare air, inhale the shimmering newness of this place: the blue water, the thick green blanket of pine, the snow-capped mountains over distant shore, with Mount Tallac a stern father. Someone had told me the lake was sacred to Native Americans; it couldn't be anything less.

The water called me. The blueness stretched out like my life, a deep yearning: I had to swim across. The idea planted itself like an indestructible seed, lingering as I descended switchbacks lined by ski runs and townhomes. With every curve, the lake presented a new face. I was in love. Bedazzled. Awed. Done for. I'd never been anywhere like this, and I discovered it my way. Alone. Nobody telling me what to think, to do, to buy, to avoid—nobody. It was mine. All mine.

I had arrived.

As seductive as the lake appeared from Kingsbury Grade, it was stony and gray up close. A quarter mile from the jetty's end, three granite sentinels jutted from the water. One-half mile north, cars barreled through Cave Rock, a granite mass blasted to form a lakeside tunnel.

I could swim to the sentinels daily, increase the distance, from my cabin. I imagined the feel of the water, gazed at the white-topped mountains, the sunlit path to Emerald Bay, and dove in.

tahoe blues

The cold shocked. Every inch of skin shrank, crawled inside. My mind locked for a moment—stunned by the frigid slice of flesh into lake—then slipped into gear. Jobs laid out by years of racing in chlorinated pools kicked in. My thighs pumped. I tucked my head, dove deeper, arms and legs extended, then burst into strokes that shot me forward, tuned my body to the test. I was a missile—impervious, invincible. The cold dimmed, though my fingers and toes remained numb.

Enervated—heart slowed, body cramped—I lost velocity. A new sensation. My throat tightened, but I gulped for air, paddled to the surface, gasped.

To warm up, allay constriction, I willed my muscles to relax, stop straining, and lengthen into fluid strokes. The smooth muscles pulled me forward. Although slower than before the fright, I was moving, breathing.

From that baptism I learned respect, and the first lesson of the lake: take her slow. You can't cheat the cold. I swam every morning. Within seconds of hitting the water, shock gave way to fluid strokes, the rocks, the path to Emerald Bay.

THREE ABOUT ECSTASY
Jeanine Stevens

We are still strangers and in no hurry. Just down from Echo Summit, we stop on the left of the highway, park and walk to where the meadow backs up to the forest. It's that kind of day where the sun is new and warm and the cool breeze lifts the branches of the dark tamaracks. Broad bands of corn lilies and monkey flowers grow close to the ground. We find ourselves waist-deep in cream-colored grass and golden-flowered cinquefoil, tall and coarse. There are meadow pools close by where mayflies bask on rush branches. All at once flurries of white butterflies settle on tips of the strongest stems. In a vortex we drop among nettles and other scratchy things not caring about cars in the distance. It must have been the mile-high elevation. We lay there after, breathless and changed.

Snow obscures broken fences and closed motels. Pilings under the dock at Ehrman Mansion leak icicles, thick and pendulous in a slow melt. I kneel on dark sand, touch water, slate blue and frothy. Later I clip the last of the lavender lilacs by the back door and place them in a pitcher on the table. The green, heart-shaped leaves ruffle and tenderly hold the scented spikes. It seems this year we missed the white one, rare and not always predictable. Later, in a full moon, we sleep on and off, tangle in and out of the sheets, get up three times to rearrange the soft muslin quilt and fluff the pillows. You doze, and I wake early to the press of the white lilac against the window, sweet, wet, and wanting.

Wanting to hike the Tahoe Rim, we begin at Spooner Summit Trailhead. The title is a little off-putting for romance, and the climb suddenly steeper than I like. As I follow and watch your hips and thighs moving, all I can think of are cedar planks, the strength of trees, and the aboriginal space we intrude upon. The trail is slippery with slick pine needles. We stop in a brief wedge of shade. You don't speak, but pull me through the trees. It seems everywhere the fleshy spikes of crimson snow plant poke up through the musky earth. The reddish scales curl back to expose the bell-shaped corollas, lobes arching over tight leaves. I accidentally knock over the largest with my boot. We bend down to where moist seeds emerge, tumble and spill into my arms.

SKYLANDIA
Laura Read

I took a visiting friend to Skylandia Park on the North Shore one June morning to walk the quarter-mile sand strip at the foot of the bluff there. She admired how the gentle waves shushed across the dark volcanic grains, and how the silver light animated the water's surface.

"You must feel very connected to this lake," she said. "Does it soothe you?"

My friend is especially responsive to nature. For her, the twenty-two-mile-long body of cerulean water and its frame of volcanic and granitic peaks were pure magic.

I am responsive to nature too, but having written news articles about the region's environmental issues for many years, for me the magic of Lake Tahoe was gone. "I used to feel a love for the lake, but now I rarely swim or have any experiences with it," I said. "The environmental problems overwhelm me. I have trouble feeling any connection at all."

She prodded for details.

"It's endless," I said. "Plumes of algae clot developed shorelines; exhaust particles drift in from the highways; nitrogen—which feeds the algae—seeps in with fertilizers from lakefront lawns. On top of that, our community fights over all of the issues: politicians croon, lawsuits mount, fees escalate. And then there's the original theft, you know, when 'we' stole Lake Tahoe from the Native Americans." I thrust my hands in the air, defeated.

My friend went quiet. I was sorry I'd spoken. I hoped I hadn't squelched her enjoyment of the place.

For months afterward, the memory of my complaints rubbed at my mind like a worn-out hat. I was tired of its scruffy torment, but what could I do?

tahoe blues

It occurred to me that my old sense of wonder might be lingering around somewhere. I could try stirring it up.

The next day I returned to Skylandia, walking the forest path and descending the steps to the beach. Sure enough, the regular strands of slimy algae fluttered like brown tissue from some boulders. My mind started its familiar churn. "Shush," I urged it. "Relax."

I stood quietly awhile, feeling awkwardly alone. The water was blue-gray, and it pulsed with small, insistent waves. The air was still. Time passed and slowed. In the sky, a couple of clouds joined up, floated together, and then drifted apart. A wind picked up and lifted the waves into curls. The ponderosas behind me stirred, reminding me of my long childhood days spent at summer camp. I removed my shoes and waded into the water. Its polar chill made my knees tremble. I splashed back onto the beach and collapsed, burrowing my hands into the sand. The pebbles warmed my fingers and chalked my skin with their dust. I felt surprisingly buzzy and fresh.

When I got home, I called my friend.

"Let's go back to Skylandia," I said. "I've found some magic I want to show you."

TAHOE MAGIC
Melissa Siig

There is something magical about Tahoe. And I'm not talking just about its ethereal beauty. Tahoe has a power about it, a mystical force that seems to draw people here and connect them. I felt it as soon as I moved to Tahoe City in 2001. Raised in the Bay Area, I had been living in Washington, DC, for six years when I decided that I was ready for a change, that I'd had enough of a city that revolved around all things serious. I spent the next five months traveling through Europe and North Africa, all the while pondering my destination when I got back to the States. My best friend kept urging me to move to Tahoe, where she had been living since she lost her job at a San Francisco start-up during the Dotcom Bust. "What the hell am I going to do in Tahoe?" I kept saying to her. But finally, when I returned from my travels shortly after 9/11, I decided to pay her a visit and see what I thought about Tahoe.

Right away, I was smitten. I felt Tahoe's magic. I loved the vibe—a community united in its love of skiing and mountain life and play. It was about as far away from Washington, DC, as you could get. I had found my tribe. And I wanted to stay.

Once I made the decision that Tahoe was my new home, things started to fall into place. Looking back, I believe it was my fate to move to Tahoe. Although it took a strange, circuitous path to get here—moving to DC, studying Middle East politics at Georgetown University, working in foreign affairs—all that somehow led me to this small ski town in the Sierra.

It also led me to the man I would marry.

I was at a coffee shop in Tahoe City when I ran into an old friend from high school. As luck would have it, we were both looking for a place to live. About a month after we moved in together,

Cheyenne's friend Siig came to visit her. I was in my pajamas. He would later tell me that he knew right away I was "the one." The thought entered my mind too, although at the time I dismissed it as being over-romantic.

But I was crazy in love. And Siig became my guide to this new world, this foreign culture that was full of language about skiing and snow I didn't understand. Our first New Year's Eve together we went to a party at High Camp at Squaw Valley. Riding up the cable car, getting my first glimpse of the mountains up close as the moonlight cast shadows below and the snow twinkled like diamonds, it felt like a fairy tale.

We were engaged six months later. I still have a note that I wrote to myself right before our wedding: "Always remember the magic."

The thing is, Tahoe never lets me forget.

ACACIA
Joan Douglas

My name is Acacia Spook, which is ironic because I'm dead.

It's so typical, isn't it? I was at a party at the lake—I watched my boyfriend making out with another girl—it made me sick and I ran. It was so dark that night I could hardly see, but I just had to get out of there. I reached the road as a car, speeding on a curve, swerved and hit me. They were drunk—the two men who panicked. They stank of beer. I recognized the man who was crying. He was my dad's fishing buddy. They freaked out and tied me up, weighed me down with fishnet loaded with stones—just chucked me in the lake like a catch that was too small.

I don't remember the beginning of my time in the lake, but that's probably for the best. I do remember watching the shore, always hoping to see my mom and dad. They came to the lake all the time when I was alive, but not anymore. I miss them.

But I'm not alone. There are quite a few of us here. There are many who've been here over a hundred years, and there are more children than you'd like to think. And so many babies. It's so sad—at least I made it to sixteen.

We don't speak to one another here. We don't have words anymore—only the ones in our heads, but they have no sound when we open our mouths. And we can't hear your chatter, your laughter, or your screams. All we hear is the lake, the trees, the wind, and the mountains.

In the winter, the water is black—I can't stand it. I leave the lake and rest among the trees above the road where I ended. I am the still of the mountain snow. The mountains hold my serenity and the lake, my wrath.

tahoe blues

In the summer, you come to the shore with your happy faces and I watch you. Your flesh glistens in the sunlight as you enrich your golden tan and I watch you. You drink your beer, your margarita, while you enjoy your sail, your party boat. I don't know why, but I am angry in the summer. I scream and scream in your face and still you throw your head back and laugh your silent laugh. You don't know how good you've got it.

You can't see me but I am the kinetic wrath of the lake.

Maybe you feel me sometimes.

Maybe you feel me when you float on the cold water.

I'm right beneath you.

I'm watching you now.

I am always watching.

Blue Lazarus
Jim Hewitt

Tangerine embers glow. My once-raging campfire has faded, dimmed to where it barely warms my feet. My campsite, reached via backpack earlier this afternoon, reveals a panorama of the entire southern half of Lake Tahoe. The translucent blue lake ringed by mountain ridges displays itself like God's footprint.

I had hiked here, set up camp, built my fire, then kicked back to watch the sun fall behind Mount Tallac. As the sun set, the baby-blue horizon shifted to crimson to deep blue to black, and the lights of the town below popped on, looking like someone sprinkled the stars across the ground. I shift my eyes from the campfire to beyond, in the distance down the mountain, the lights of the Tahoe casino corridor resembling campfire embers.

A campfire is like a crystal ball; if you stare into it, let the focus drift from your eyes, and allow your mind to float, the past, present, and future will appear to you. The present, or recent past, appears in the coals of my fire. Last night, as I drove into the casino corridor, I turned from an empty street into an empty parking garage, then walked through an empty casino. A solitary blackjack dealer flipped her cards at a solitary gambler. Music played for nobody as a bartender wiped down the video poker machines at his empty bar.

In the campfire, the image of the present is replaced by one of the past: gamblers perched at every slot machine, revelers hip-to-hip crowding every blackjack table, nightclubs filled to capacity, a fleet of taxis at the Tahoe airport waiting for gamblers, partiers, and vacationers. Tahoe was *the* place to holiday on the West Coast—Monte Carlo in the mountains. Fifteen years ago, Tahoe casinos employed more than twenty thousand people; now it's less than five thousand. Streams of money from gamblers, partiers, and tourists bolstered an economy that permitted locals to live well in such a spectral place. Over time, the casino economy has dimmed to embers.

As I exited the parking garage last night, I looked over my shoulder at a marquee: "Bethany, One Woman Show." A fitting image: Bethany was the town where Christ resurrected Lazarus from the dead. I turned the corner behind Harveys casino, down a block of motels, some boarded up, some run down. A five-block abandoned excavation marked a failed attempt to resurrect the local economy. The Lazarus neighborhood.

Looking into the fire, I try to discern the future. What will stoke the embers of Tahoe so it once again will rage? The image of the future I see is the lake, pristine, glorious, and independent. The lake does not need tourists, does not need casinos, does not need an economy.

The lake needs not a resurrection.

VIII

slate

The Plague
DJ DeProspero

Maricel begins her day looking out the window, as if something will have changed overnight to make things better. The bright-blue sky shines off the dark, murky sludge that fills the lake. Hard to believe it used to be a deep, clear blue, she thinks. No one living remembers that; they've just seen the old, faded posters promoting Keep Tahoe Blue. Guess that didn't work.

Nothing has changed. Today will be the same as every other day now—hot and long. She'd better get started. She falls on her knees in front of the altar nearest her bed. She prays to the Virgin Mary, Our Lady of Guadalupe, Krishna, God, Mother Nature, Buddha, Jesus, Joseph, Ganesha, other gods she's heard of, trees, flowers, bees, rocks, and anything and anyone else she thinks might, just might, offer some assistance.

When she can't think of anyone else to appeal to, or when she's reached the end of the row of altars in her room (it's a small room so the number of altars is limited—most are multipurpose), she gets off her knees and gets dressed for work. She grabs her bow and quiver of arrows and heads out the door.

Maricel is convinced that she escaped the 2017 plague because she was away at church camp when her brother got sick. She tried to convince her mother and sister to leave San Francisco then. They thought things would get better and staying put was the best thing to do. By the time the 2023 flu epidemic was raging, she had given up trying to convince them to join her in Meyers, where she had gone to live with her guru. It was too late anyway. Two years ago the Tahoe Governors initiated the Walls Project to keep Bay Area escapees from coming in. She knows she's lucky to be here and to have a job.

tahoe blues

The quiver is empty when she comes in the door at night and again falls on her knees in front of the Mother Nature altar. She's tired and hungry but knows what she has to do first. She moves along the row, thanking idol after idol for not making her kill anyone she knew today.

THE WORKER
Cleo Fellers Kocol

I paint houses in the Tahoe region. California or Nevada, lakeside or higher up, I tackle the area's biggest, fanciest, costliest vacation homes. No watered-down paint, no cheap substitutes, and I mix my own colors. My two helpers and I wear plastic booties, pure white painters' clothes, and I smile. "Yes, sir," I say. And, "No, sir, no problem, we'll use the facilities in the guesthouse." Jobs today are few.

This guy, Franklin Robertson, who retired as a CEO on Wall Street, eyes my helpers and says before we start, "That one with the mustache, he related to Pancho Villa?"

I play it straight. "No, sir, he isn't. His daddy came from Greece. He was born here."

He nods and shrugs. "Can't be too careful these days."

"No, sir, you can't."

I feel that place on the back of my neck ease as Robertson leaves the room. I check, find I have enough paint to finish the job, catch the master suite later. His wife sleeps days. She's the current act at Harrah's. Marcus and I caught the early show last Saturday. She's blonde, fragile, and has pipes that would soothe the devil. I try not to think about the paunch that Robertson can't suck in. I can't picture them together.

I finish the trim while Marcus and Adam do the great room. Robertson sits on the deck oiling his rifles, ramrod, cloth, and oil at hand, a radio running full blast. A talk show host slams the economy and suggests workers take a cut in pay. "Make it easier for employers to hire more workers." A caller protests. The host retaliates. "Don't you think we all should sacrifice like 'the greatest generation' did in World War II?" Patriotic music swells in the background.

Robertson hollers "Amen" and turns the volume up. I gather Mrs. Robertson sleeps through anything.

At noon she comes down belting a terrycloth robe. "Two more nights," I hear her say. "The Salsa Señoritas follow me and will do an introductory set at my last show."

Robertson's expression of superiority slides into place. "Who in hell are the Salsa whatevers?" He looks up from the Remington he's cleaning.

She stares through the open door to the back deck where I sit eating my sandwich. She's barefoot, and her hair is tied back in a ponytail. "A rock group. They're high on the charts." Her eyes meet mine.

I feel that tug of recognition. We share a generation.

Robertson mutters and looks straight at her. "Stupid kid music."

Biting her lip, she leaves.

The radio host suggests that maybe too many regulations force employers to hire illegal workers.

Robertson says, "He's got that right," and looks to me for confirmation.

I say, "Yes, sir," again. Returning, dressed and made up now, she glances my way and smiles. I want to smile back, protect her. I don't. I take no chances, and I hate myself for it.

THE TIME WE HAD
Ryan Row

I was in the timeless place behind the counter at Ski Run Liquor Market, with the cigarettes and the hard bottles. The little liquor store with the flickering florescent lights and dust-filmed neons in the windows. It's by the pawnshop and the CVS and one of those nameless, weekly rate motel places where families live in the off-seasons. Time didn't really pass in there. The shift would start and the shift would end, but time never made itself apparent in between. The same guy came in for the same tall can of Mickey's four or five times in the same, short six-hour shift.

"You could buy them all at once, you know," I said one night, a long time ago. Before I knew.

"Naw, I'd just drink them all that way." That made a certain kind of sense in the beyond-white light there, which hides as much as it shows. He winked at me as he left, and time continued to not move.

The homeless are also frequent patrons. One took a strange liking to me. He smelled of dirt and oil. Heavy clothes. He had pink headphones that played static loud enough to hear a few feet away. I never saw him without them.

He came in one almost-night, when the sun was setting some amazing color or another, pink or purple or orange, over the lake and snowy mountains. He grunted and spat sounds of disbelief, and his body twitched all over.

I didn't ask. He may have liked me, but I didn't like him, or really any person while I sold smoke and colored water.

"Would you ever beg for money?" When he spoke it was like an engine backfiring, short and loud. Without waiting for an answer, "No. You never would. You have pride."

"I don't know," I said, "If I had to, I might."

"No. No you wouldn't. God."

"I guess not."

"I understand hard times, He knows I do, but you never beg."

"I guess."

"I know. I worked in a state mental institution. And they told me the first day, they told me, 'This will either make you or break you.' And I know it broke me."

I didn't know what to say to that, so I didn't say anything. My face like a field of snow.

That may have pissed him off a little. His red face may have gotten redder.

"God. You don't know. We have a, a disconnect, you and me," he had said. He couldn't make a fist, could only half curl his weather-swollen hand like a drying aspen leaf in fall.

His obituary was in the Sunday *Tribune*. He had a wife and a teenage boy.

Reading that just made me tired. Yeah, we're tired as the whole earth around here. But morning never comes, and we never sleep. It's always almost night. For some of us time has stopped.

A Means to Survive
Gloria Sinibaldi

They come in cars, busses, and airplanes to commune with nature and bathe in Tahoe's majestic glory. Here they can fish, swim, hike, and bike, though it's winter sports that provide the biggest attraction. These adventure seekers look forward to flying off Tahoe's mountaintops like birds with newfound wings. So passionate is their quest for this lifestyle that one vital detail is often overlooked—a means to survive.

So they come to the One Stop Job Resource Center for a solution to this dilemma, their ski caps hanging loose, no pen in hand. Some haul in snowboards and stash them in the corner.

"Can you find me a job?"

"What kind of job are you looking for?"

"Anything," the standard reply.

"Do you have a résumé?"

"Nope, don't need one. Whaddya have available?"

"You will conduct a self-directed job search," I tell the inquirer. "You will attend a job search workshop for help and important tips," I say, handing him a schedule. "Once you're registered you can use the center's resources."

"My friend's waitin' in the car," the man says, shifting nervously and eyeing the room. "No time for that."

"Did you bring your work documents?" I ask him.

"Nope … lost my wallet, but my papers are packed in a box somewhere. My name's Blake."

"Well, Blake, you'll need them when you find a job."

"I'll bring 'em tomorrow, okay?"

Seated at a computer to register for work, Blake is clearly out of his element. Others like him are crazed keyboarders, ready to check

tahoe blues

this task off their lists as quickly as possible. The result, however, is the same—no jobs. Eventually, a collective sigh of despair hangs overhead.

"I'm couch surfin' again tonight. Ain't no jobs out there!" Blake laments.

"How long ya been here?" the listener next to him inquires.

"'Bout two months," he replies, wiping his face with his sleeve. "You had any luck?"

"Nada. I screwed up my knee at Heavenly, and my brother's been payin' my rent. His wife is pissed! Unemployment's run out, so now I'm on food stamps." He rifles through a stack of dog-eared papers stuffed in his backpack. "Been working construction since I was fifteen. Ain't never been this bad!"

"Computers suck," Blake mumbles, lost in his own abyss. "Before, you could get a job on a handshake. Now you hafta screw around with these damned things."

"Yep... bummer," the reply.

United in sobering reality, the two depart together, shoulders slumped, faces long. Blake grumbles something about "being an American." His new buddy nods and clenches his fist in agreement. They board the BlueGo bus going west on Highway 50.

CHAIN MONKEY
Bruce Rettig

Ice chunks the size of cinder blocks form a wall across the end of the driveway. Dave Bradley rubs at the pain underneath the creases of his forehead. Son of a bitch—why doesn't that damn snowplow driver raise the blade when he comes by? Dave climbs into his rusted-out pickup and warms up the engine. "The hell with shoveling," he says to himself, guns the engine, and bounces over the snow berm and into the street. Tire tracks glisten in the glow of headlights.

He stops at Roadrunner for coffee and leaves the motor running. Blue-colored exhaust billows out of the tailpipe.

"Mornin', Dave."

"Mornin'."

"I didn't see you at Steamers Friday night. You work things out with Jenny?"

"Nope. She left town." Dave pours the brew into a Styrofoam cup, then sets a couple of bills on the counter.

"Sorry to hear that."

"Don't be." Dave grabs the change and walks out the door. The coffee washes the lump from his throat but doesn't help the headache. Maybe one more beer before bed last night wasn't such a good idea.

There's a line of cars waiting at the checkpoint when he drives up and opens his door. The leg zipper on his coverall is blown apart so he wraps it with duct tape. A twentysomething wearing a "chain crew" vest walks over.

"Hey Dave."

"Hey Mike."

"Runnin' late this morning?"

"Yep."

tahoe blues

The first vehicle Dave chains up is a minivan, family of five. There's a dog in the back, tongue smudges across the rear window. Dave had a helluva dog when he was a kid—part of the family, and they spoiled him like crazy.

The next vehicle is a black Lexus. The guy's wearing a top-of-the-line Descente jacket, and his girlfriend looks about half his age.

"I'm in a hurry. Big meeting tomorrow, you know how it—" The man looks at Dave's duct-taped coveralls. "An extra ten if you're fast."

Dave lays out the chains but they're too long. "Hey Mike, give me a hand will ya? And bring the tools." They shorten the chains and fasten them on the tires.

The Lexus's window opens. "I didn't expect it to take that long."

"They were the wrong size—had to shorten 'em."

"They're brand new." The man hands over a folded twenty, minus the ten-spot. The window shuts and Dave is separated from the driver by a layer of tinted glass. Dave raises his fist, but a flash of light stops him.

The sun breaks the horizon and paints the peaks in a fiery light. For a moment, maybe not more than a few seconds, he hears nothing but the faint sound of wind rushing over the mountaintops. The family's minivan pulls onto the highway, and the dog looks out the back window, tongue hanging out, small fingers rubbing its ears.

"Hey, you all right?" Mike waves his hand in front of Dave.

"No," he pauses, "but I will be."

SNOW MECHANICS
Stacy Hicks

I stepped out the door, into the hush of a wintry November night. The cup of coffee in my hand steaming through the small hole in the lid. Cars clank slowly by on the road, fifty feet away. I go down the stairs and turn to my right, following the frozen ruts of tires, vehicles long since passed. At the end of the building sits a truck parked beneath a tree and half buried in the falling snow, the hood up, metal clanking against metal echoing out. An umbrella, inside out, handle stuck in the snow bank, leans to the left. The orange glow of the portable propane heater emits a meager heat. The liquid guts of the truck have been poured out, and the snow has melted away to bare, wet asphalt, visible in the glint of the dim flashlight that sits on the engine. I stand there as the man talks to himself, alternately cussing and purring at the difficult bolt that won't thread on.

I set the cup of coffee down on the engine and turn around, resting against the cold metal body. High up above, in a sky a thousand miles deep and wide, hangs the moon. Shining down, turning night into day, stars scattered like buckshot, dimples puncturing the blackness all around. The lake glows still and gentle under the light, untold mysteries within its cool waters. The cold starts to numb my face. I stamp my feet and rub my hands together. I can't imagine how the man standing over the engine feels. His hands are bare and black, covered in oil and grease. I don't need to be here, but the silence of the night calls to me, telling me to enjoy the solitude. Earlier in the evening, he had pulled me outside. His body beckoning me to follow him onto the back porch. "Have you seen the moon? Have you been outside tonight? Come see." His eager face lit up the darkness of the room. I laughed and followed, the sound of my flip-flops smacking across the wooden floor.

On the porch, my toes are bare and cold, turning red amidst the white. The stillness of the world under a fresh snowfall is an incredible thing to behold. Everything is less hurried, everything seems to breathe slower, and everything has been transformed. No longer am I surrounded by recognizable objects: strange creatures now lurk around the corner, and Dr. Seuss–like structures reach into the clear night. Your breath sings out, warm air hitting cold air, glasses fogging up. Trees no longer talk, and icicles form off the roof, as thick as your arm, dripping, freezing, and forever moving down till they meet the ground. Close your eyes and hear the world whisper to you; you will never be the same.

DEALERS
Daniel Ward

I just got back from a weekend in Tahoe dealing on the North Shore, shaving and brushing my teeth in the woods, sleeping and studying in my car. I was getting ready for work and realized I didn't have my casino dress shoes. I backtracked and found them in the parking lot at Spooner Summit, where I'd stood outside my Toyota in the middle of the night and taken them off along with my black pants and button-down shirt, which I put on a hanger in my car. After putting on some jeans, I'd gotten back into my car without the shoes. I was so relieved when I drove to the spot and, despite all of the daytime boat inspection activity, there they were, one standing upright and the other lying on its side, patiently waiting for my return.

I always park in the middle of a parking lot so nothing can come up on me. The previous summer, car in the shop and hitching toward Tahoe City in the small hours, a bear came out of the trees, first pacing on my right, then drifting behind and following for about a hundred yards. Bears look warm and fuzzy during the day, but when there's a coal-black silhouette with nothing between you and it but a single lane of asphalt, it's a different story. I could have asked a friend for a weekend couch, but who likes to ask for help, especially when you need it. Besides, I often didn't have enough gas to go to the South Shore and get back to work the following night.

My first casino job in 1983, I had a full-time position, five paid sick days, *paid* medical insurance in sixty days, regular raises, and a twenty-minute break every hour. If you find a dealer like that now, take a picture. Dealers take more abuse than anyone else in the casino. The players are angry when they lose, the bosses when they win, and—nose picking, arguing, spitting, sneezing, cursing,

cheating, smoking, coughing, farting, yelling, and belching aside—
there is occasionally a little unpleasantness:

A gambler says that if he doesn't win the next hand, he'll
shoot himself. He doesn't win the next hand. He shoots himself. A
gambler fails to notice that he's ignited his hair and continues to hit.
A gambler ignores the dealer's betting instructions one more time.
The dealer takes the man in a headlock and bangs his head into
the ATM again and again. A gambler hits a dealer in the eye with
a silver dollar giving her a black eye. A gambler wins a fortune and
offers the dealer a Kennedy half. The dealer tosses it back, hitting
the gambler in the forehead between the eyes. A gambler can't cash
a check. He drives his backhoe through the plate glass doors. An
infuriated dealer offers a gambler a hundred dollars simply to not
play on his game. The dealer is reported and reduced to writing this
piece.

IX

midnight

THE KEEPERS
Erica Olsen

In the humidification chamber the paper takes up water vapor from the outer basin. Over the course of a few hours it relaxes visibly—the tight and brittle roll loosens, then unrolls itself. With my encouragement, the edge of the map, now pliable, opens like the petal of a flower, and after a few hours I can spread it out without fear of cracking the paper and see, for the first time, what I'm looking at: a map from the 2030s that came to us recently from a private collection. As always with such maps, I am astonished, first at the survival of the paper, and then at the size of the lake. Our institute— the library and archives, the reading room, the exhibit gallery—is located here, where the blue of Crystal Bay ripples beneath my index finger, a spot that in those days was beneath several hundred feet of water.

I'm a conservator. My specialty is paper. I have a colleague who catalogs, one who curates exhibitions, another whose responsibility is the migration of data. We are the keepers of the lake—of the memory of the lake. We keep maps, photographs (though it's impossible to be sure of the authenticity of these images), drawings, paper records of all kinds, audiovisual materials, the whole range of items that are evidence of the former existence of this place. In the old days, I've been told, geologists used to come quite often to do research at the institute, as did climate change researchers, and wildlife biologists. The scientists have moved on to other cataclysms. These days, though we don't like to admit it, we get mostly the antiquarians.

After the lowering of the Sierra Nevada and the transformation (more rapid than anticipated) of the lake into seasonal wetlands and a vast, grassy meadow surrounding a small pond, the institute was founded, retroactively, to document the lake's natural and cultural history. We do what we can, with a budget courtesy of several generous donors.

This particular map must have been the work of an artist, I observe as I spread it between sheets of blotting paper to flatten and dry. Its beauty is excessive, beyond the needs of cartographic function. It was printed with techniques that were antique even then, on paper made of cotton not wood pulp (in order, I realize with sudden, grateful understanding, to survive for us, the keepers). You can see the first noticeable alterations in the shoreline, the bays filling in, the silting.

I work in the lab all morning. In the afternoon I take a walk on one of the meadow trails that crisscross our institute grounds, where, each spring, some migratory birds persist in returning. Just now a golden-brown merganser came in for a landing at the edge of the meadow then flew on, with a confused flapping, to take refuge in the willow marsh where a small body of shallow water remains, for how long we do not know.

LAKE VIEW
Scott A. Lukas

Perhaps the truth depends on a walk around the lake.
—Wallace Stevens

When we walk around the Lake, we are urged to reflect on its inherent value—its beauty, its ability to connect us, its way of granting us relaxation from the chaos. Anything less than a complete affirmation of *it* may be seen as an act of heresy. Imagine if this conversation took place: "Wow, isn't this an amazing view?" "Not really, it's the same lake that it has always been. It's really not that amazing a view; it's quite ordinary." The second person would likely be thrown to the bottom of the Lake. When we hike with a friend or loved one to the top of Pyramid Peak or Mount Tallac, we are asked to pause, to look down, and to simply take the Lake in, to appreciate *it*, to simply let *it* be. This view of the Lake and the essence of all that *it* entails has come to mean the greatest of all values, and the Lake, in turn, has become the greatest of all religions, for *it* is never seen as such and thus *it* is granted real power. And it should be valued; it is, after all, the one thing that, through all the differences of the onlookers who use it for a variety of reasons, remains what *it* is—a lake. Yet, at the same time, when we look at the Lake we forget that the meaning of *view* is a "formal inspection or survey." There is nothing to inspect while staring at its blue, and even with the introspection that it inspires and how perhaps it changes us, changes our course, we so often fall back on the conformity that it provides us.

Wallace Stevens was prescient when he wrote of the way that a lake could facilitate the truth, but when we let it become the sole facilitator, we are further from the truth. For so long we have looked at the Lake and have assumed that we are acting on its behalf. Every glance at it, every dip in it, every splash of it is an act in homage to *it*. The Lake, like the greater nature that encompasses it, is seen as a sign, in and of itself. In the ultimate apotheosis, the Lake is given a supremacy that none of the glancers, dippers, and splashers can overcome. It simply *is*. And because *it is*, we assume that there is nothing that we could ever do—whether we gamble away our savings, addict ourselves to death, beat up our spouse, or pollute a random lake—that would take away from what *it is*. By naming it, we make claim to empowering it, but we cannot have our Lake and eat it too. The only way to give the Lake its agency back is to no longer name it, to no longer glance at it, to leave *it* completely behind.

Lapin a la Moutarde
Liz Tucker

They said he was the killer, that he cooked his own girlfriend. Skinned alive, and quartered! I think differently. Yet, I never told the full story.

Theirs was a love of rabbit stew, marinating high in the mountains for years in a rich mustard sauce of affection, braised over thyme with mutual adoration, and served on a communal bed of sautéed cabbage. I should know, because I had the pleasure of spending a weekend at their cabin last winter.

We took early morning walks, identifying silent tracks of racoons, coyote, snowshoe hares. He pointed out sitzmarks, imprints left in the snow by animals falling from above. I hoped to see grizzly tracks, but I was told they no longer lived in the Sierra.

"Last one killed in '22," she said with a grin. I felt vulnerable. I felt a fool.

"But it's on your state flag," I argued. She just hunched her shoulders and closed her eyes.

Later, we snowshoed the Rubicon trail. It was steep and unnerving. He took the lead, pointing out Slide Mountain, Spooner Summit, Lake Tahoe below. I braced myself. I didn't want to look down, but he shamed me. *Don't be a chicken, Ted. Drink it in. You'll never see anything like it.* So I did. And it was true—the cobalt waters were stunning. "A ferocious beauty," I declared. I could see down into her soul, where wide boulders of truth lay at the heart of it all. They were solid and unmoving, bearing witness to eons of geologic turmoil. Later I thought to myself, he could have thrown me over, but he didn't.

Over dinner, we watched evening fall into night. Just as quickly as the winter sky faded from the Carson Range, the lake had left us completely alone. We looked into the darkness and cheered our good fortune. He grabbed her, and together they stood on his chair, arm in arm, looking out to where the lake once lay moments before.

"I'm in live!" he yelled. I thought he meant to say "in love," but he didn't. He was *in live*, and I had never seen anybody more so.

There were toasts of red wine and an unabashed zesting of lust. Right there at the table. It was unmistakable. While others hibernated during the long winter months, those two snowshoe hares were quite active. They screwed, well, like rabbits. All night. And like I said, right there at the table. It was a thing of beauty. They left undeniable sitzmarks throughout the cabin, and when I walked back to the car the next morning, I found them everywhere. Alive and deeply imbedded in the new layer of snow that fell overnight.

So to all those who shake their boorish fingers declaring he did it, I say everybody should be so lucky. Lucky to simmer for hours, if not years, to their Crock-Potted deaths in the arms of such a brazen lover high above the dark, still waters of that inimitable lake.

DESOLATION
John Q. McDonald

"There's one."

"Another."

"How many you got so far?"

"I'm up to two seventy-five."

"I've got three hundred."

"We can compare notes in the morning."

"You sure you want to go on that hike?"

"Sure, it'll be fun."

"But your kind of fun always wears me out."

"You've never been to the Desolation Wilderness. You'll love it."

There was a pause in the warm darkness as we continued to count meteors in the summer sky. We were at a cabin uphill from the lake, and not far from the wilderness. I stood with my neck craned. He reclined on a pad spread out on a rock. The Perseid meteor shower was more of a trickle, but we were counting more than we usually saw. No storm, but it was a good year.

"I'm not exactly in great shape for a hike these days," I said. I counted, too, my chins and the number of times, on one hand, that I'd gone on a long hike.

"You'll be fine. I'll go easy on you."

"That's what you said last time. It took me days to recover."

"Good for ya."

"Yeah, I suppose that's true."

The summer sky wheeled silently overhead, sparking with the intermittent shooting stars—each one a glint of light always seeming to come from the corner of my eye. I turned to look, as if the meteor would still be there, and I dwelled on that patch of sky, as if there would be another right there at any moment. The sky didn't work that way. We were surely counting many of the same meteors, and we exclaimed together if we both saw one of particular brightness.

"Desolation Wilderness," I said. "Sounds redundant." Gold Rush travelers and miners utterly lost in the mountains, somehow missing the glittering expanse of the great lake, naming the stark granite for their sense of hopelessness and loss.

"Oh, nice one," he said. "But a sporadic, not a Perseid."

"Hardly matters."

"You're not counting the sporads, are you?"

"Well, yes."

"Not an accurate count." He was cut short by a greenish streak in the south. "I'm not publishing my results, just enjoying the meteors."

"Then why count at all?"

"Keep talking and you'll lose count yourself."

There was a silence of several minutes. Five more meteors burned out overhead. We could almost see by the starlight. I felt my irises reaching for light in the darkness.

"Desolation," I said.

"Desolation," he said.

Wanderers lost in the mountains. A wilderness. The indifferent black sky. The glints of forgotten dust vaporizing in the thin air. Standing there, looking up, feeling like an isolated, tiny, and empty thing.

But it felt right, somehow. Just right.

There was a blaze of light, and the trees for an instant cast sharp shadows against the pale rock. We gasped at the fireball. The landscape fell back into darkness, and a faint glowing trail lingered in the sky. A path with no beginning and no end.

THE ORBIT OF KNOWN OBJECTS
Lisa Veyssiere

I am fourteen, and here is Orion—or no, it's a calamity of aircraft, or no, not even that, just a funny little satellite to one of the minor stars. Or looking down, into the lake, a mirror reflection of starshine, or jet fuel, or the electrified dust of the cosmos. We are in the ninth grade, and nobody knows yet that the universe is flinging itself apart, but we do know that the lake is deep, deeper than anyone can measure, except the navy. We suspect the navy is hiding out in Campsite 13, disguised as sophomores who possess outrageous talent with guitars. *Orion*, I insist, to the proclamation of *absolutely not*. The daughters of the biology teacher learn the proper name of the galaxy, the nomenclature for *Pyrrharctia isabella*, a moth the exact color of the velvet skirt I wore to the Shoreline Amphitheatre the week before, the measurable depth of Lake Tahoe, and the second law of thermodynamics. The importance of Easter vacation has nothing on a big bang thirty-four billion years ago. We brush our teeth in the slimy bathroom, listen to the singsong of songbirds in the Sierra Nevada before lunch. The jay population reproduces with the seasonal maturation of nuts from the pinion pines.

"The origin of all things that matter," I say. *Just matter*, he corrects me. As in: hard rock. "Oh shiny sentiment of star fall," I whisper. *Sediment*, he says, shale, obsidian, gypsum. To learn the secret of history, you must first pay attention to the natural history of granite and understand geologic time. I don't quite listen. What daughter wants to hear her father differentiate rocks? I dream of a field guide to the living birds and that Jeremy, who keeps a Camel soft pack in his JanSport, drops spiders into my mouth as I sleep. From Campsite 13, riffs of "Stella Blue" mingle with the brown moths outside the trailer door.

And twenty-three years later it's the same star fall but new ash scattering: the complexities of daughterhood, orphanhood. Campsite 13 is occupied by a Modelo bottle and a family of quail, and it's a funny thing, something I understand about as well as the orbit of known objects: these ashes of you, the aged body of me, the descendants of that velvet burnout moth, the pinion pine, even the asphalt on Highway 50, all composed of the differentiated particulate of unknown objects, flung so far from their predecessor, that origin of all things—matter.

Dana Arlien, MD, is a physician residing in Incline Village with her husband, Jon, and dog, Harry. She received her bachelor of science in neurobiology, physiology, and behavior from the University of California, Davis, graduating with honors. Dana then attended the University of Nevada School of Medicine where she completed her residency in adult psychiatry and her fellowship in child and adolescent psychiatry. Dana is currently the chief of staff at Willow Springs Center, a residential treatment center for children and adolescents in Reno, Nevada. She has a strong interest in working with children and adolescents who have been victims of trauma and abuse. In her spare time, Dana enjoys trail running, equestrian sports, kayaking, Nordic skiing, yoga, and CrossFit, and loves the adventure of traveling to new places. Having a strong appreciation for art, Dana says she writes because "I can't paint."

Joan Atkinson has lived in Northern Nevada for more than thirty years and is still amazed at how bitterly cold Lake Tahoe is. When she's not riding herd on two lawyers at her top-secret day job, she and hubby Frank are hiking, biking, or skiing, usually within a hundred-mile radius of her home. Joan's work has appeared in regional magazines and newspapers, and she wrote about beer (!) as a columnist for *Rocky Mountain Brewing News*. www.joanatkinson.com

Charlotte Austin holds a bachelor of arts in environmental science from the University of Washington and is currently a master's candidate at the University of Alaska, Anchorage. When she's not writing, her work as a mountain guide takes her around the globe. She lives in Seattle, Washington.

Alison Bender is a freelance writer and editor. A graduate of Penn State University, she moved west in 2005, living in San Francisco, Rocklin, and Truckee before settling in Reno, Nevada. She now resides at the foot of Mt. Rose with her husband, Jason, daughter, Nora Kathleen, and furry best friend, Cassie. A longtime former editor at *Tahoe Quarterly* magazine, she loves reading and writing about the Tahoe region; her favorite places include Lake Tahoe's East Shore beaches and the Mt. Rose Wilderness. She also enjoys writing about travel, architecture, pregnancy, and parenting. www. alisonobender.com

Mary Cook, a native Upstate New Yorker, holds a bachelor's degree in biology from Cornell University. Her love for skiing spawned from three years of ski instructing at Heavenly Mountain Resort. Mary's poems have been published in *The Kokanee*. Currently, she works as a freelance development editor for nursing textbooks and tutors college students in writing. Mary lives in South Lake Tahoe with her boyfriend and dog.

Erin Costello is a poet and digital artist. After spending a few years living in South Lake Tahoe, she moved to Boulder, Colorado, to earn an MFA in creative writing from the University of Colorado. Her work has appeared recently in various journals and venues including *Trickhouse* and *Drunken Boat*. She is the cofounder of SpringGun Press and lives in Denver, Colorado.

Kimberly Covill was born and raised in rural New Hampshire. She now lives most of the year out West, but still uses the word "wicked" whenever possible. Kimberly graduated from St. Lawrence University in Upstate New York in 2006. While in school, she played rugby and spent a semester abroad in East Africa. When she was twenty-two, Kimberly drove cross-country to California, where she got a job traveling the state as an outdoor educator. She spent the next five winters living at Lake Tahoe and skiing in the Sierra. Summers find her kayaking rivers in the Northeast. Kimberly lives with her boyfriend in Montana and is learning to horseback ride.

Mojie Crigler writes fiction, memoir, and plays. Her work has appeared in *Drunken Boat*, *Critical Flame*, *Los Angeles Review*, and elsewhere. Her story "How the Film *Flint* Distorts the Truth" received the 2010 Howard Frank Mosher Short Fiction Prize and was published in *Hunger Mountain*.

DJ DeProspero is a Bay Area resident who loves reading good writing and occasionally gives it a try herself.

Joan Douglas was born in Iowa, lived in Nebraska till ten, Hawaii till twenty-three, San Francisco for twenty years until the English countryside beckoned. Settled in Lake Tahoe now—till death do they part.

Stefanie Freele is the twice Pushcart Prize–nominated author of the short story collection *Feeding Strays* (Lost Horse Press), and a finalist in the John Gardner Binghamton University Fiction Award and the Book of the Year Award. She recently won the Glimmer Train Fiction Open. Her published and forthcoming work can be found in *Glimmer Train*, *Sou'wester*, *The Florida Review*, *American Literary Review*, *Night Train*, *Whitefish Review*, *EDGE*, *Sierra Nevada Review*, *Pank*, and *Word Riot*. Stefanie is the fiction editor of the *Los Angeles Review*. Stefanie's second collection, *Surrounded by Water*, will be published by Press 53 in 2012. She has an MFA in creative writing from the Northwest Institute of Literary Arts – Whidbey Writers Workshop.

Margaret Elysia Garcia lives as a mountain woman in the northern Sierra Nevada, though she hails from Los Angeles. She writes for ParentingSquad.com and its sister blog WiseBread.com and has become their alternative parent/rural crazy person.

Tim Hauserman wrote the official guidebook to the Tahoe Rim Trail, as well as *Monsters in the Woods: Backpacking with Children* and *Cross-Country Skiing in the Sierra Nevada*. His articles have appeared in *Backpacker*, *Cross-Country Skier*, *High Country News*, *Nevada Magazine*, *Reno Magazine*, and a number of other publications. His column "Growing Up in Tahoe" regularly appears in *Moonshine Ink*. He teaches cross-country skiing and directs the Strider-Gliders after-school ski program at Tahoe Cross Country Ski Area in Tahoe City.

Jim Hewitt grew up with dreams of becoming a novelist, only to allow life to step on those plans. Putting down the pen, he lived *vox silentium* for ten years. He is back, fervently writing to catch up on those lost years.

Stacy Hicks lives in Strawberry, California, with her son, Caine. A photographer as well as a writer, she finds inspiration all around her, being lucky enough to live in truly amazing areas. She was born and raised around Seattle and the Hood Canal in Washington state, and attended school at Western Washington University, graduating with a BA in history and a minor in criminology.

David Higginbotham is a writer and professor at Hampden Sydney College. He lives in Central Virginia with his wife and son.

Jim Hildinger is a lifelong resident of the Lake Tahoe Basin. He received his master's degree in music education with a minor in the natural sciences from Los Angeles State College. In 1958 he was employed as a music teacher by the Lake Tahoe Unified School District and retired from that job in 1987. During the past twenty years he has become well known in the Tahoe area for his large black-and-white images, which are produced with both medium- and large-format cameras. Vistas of scenic beauty are a favorite challenge for him, but he also enjoys using his skills and equipment to produce architectural essays. During the summer he is busy with a family resort. In the winter he sails his Catalina 27 on Lake Tahoe, carries his forty pounds of cameras around the mountains of the Tahoe area, and enjoys the luxury of deciding what to do with his time.

His environmental philosophy is easy to determine from his frequent statement that "the best possible thing that you could do for Lake Tahoe is to go away and leave it alone; the environment cannot compromise—it can only react." In his next breath, however, Jim can evoke Frank Lloyd Wright as he dreams of a future where, with proper planning, many more people could conceivably enjoy the natural splendors of the Tahoe area without additional environmental impact.

Shawn Huestis was born and raised in South Lake Tahoe, California, where he has lived for all twenty-five years of his life. He has a 160-pound English mastiff named Toby. He has an identical twin brother who is a specialist in the US Army, and recently returned from a year tour in Afghanistan. Shawn is fascinated by the human mind, and is majoring in psychology. He started working for the El Dorado County Department of Mental Health when he was nineteen years old. He currently performs suicide risk assessments and suicide interventions in the South Lake Tahoe area. His interests include: hiking, weight lifting, reading, and writing. Shawn is currently working on a novel titled *The Furies*. He plans on becoming a marriage and family therapist, and a published author.

Writing stories, novels, and poetry, as well as giving historical talks at various venues, keeps **Cleo Fellers Kocol** busy. She began freelancing at age fifty-one; she's now eighty-five. She wrote and performed in three one-woman, many-character shows she presented throughout the country in the 1980s. Her fiction won various prizes, including the Wilmer Culver Memorial Award for fiction and nonfiction. Her poetry has been set to music and danced at the Palace of the Legion of Honor in San Francisco. She was named Humanist Heroine in 1988 by the American Humanist Organization. She has been a teacher of creative writing and is now an active member of the Renaissance Society at California State University, Sacramento.

Elisabeth Korb is an Atlanta, Georgia, native and a seven-year North Tahoe resident. A freelance editor and copywriter by profession, she dabbles in journalism and creative writing and moonlights as a block printer. She is the former managing editor of *Tahoe Quarterly* magazine and web editor of Tahoe Mountain Sports, and her current clients include the Center for Basque Studies at the University of Nevada, Reno; Bona Fide Books; The Child's World; Smith + Jones; and *Moonshine Ink*, for which she writes a bimonthly arts column. Her editing work spans all genres, from the political memoir of Juan José Ibarretxe, the former president of the Basque Country, to the poetry collection of Jason Schossler, winner of the 2010 Melissa Lanitis Gregory Poetry Prize. Follow her

tahoe blues

writing, editing, crafting endeavors, and postcard collection at www. blanksmith.com and www.28cents.tumblr.com.

Krista Lukas was born in Truckee, California, and grew up at Lake Tahoe. She received her bachelor of arts in literature from University of California, San Diego, in 1992. She serves as the gifted and talented specialist at Jacks Valley and Zephyr Cove Elementary Schools in Douglas County, Nevada, where she lives with her husband, Scott.

Her poem "Letter from My Ancestors" was selected by guest editor Billy Collins for inclusion in *The Best American Poetry 2006*. The same poem appears in the textbook *Creative Writer's Handbook*, the anthology *New Poets of the American West*, and in Russian translation in *Polutona Magazine*. Krista is the recipient a 2007 Nevada Arts Council Fellowship and the 2008 Robert Gorrell Award for Literary Achievement.

Scott A. Lukas (PhD Rice University, cultural anthropology) is a professor of anthropology and sociology at Lake Tahoe Community College. In addition to his work on the Gender Ads Project, he is the author/editor of five books, including collections on popular culture. He was also a contributor to the *Handbook for Achieving Gender Equity through Education* and the *Routledge International Encyclopedia of Men and Masculinities*. His most recent book is *Theme Park* published with Reaktion Books. He has been recognized with the McGraw-Hill Award for Excellence in Undergraduate Teaching of Anthropology by the American Anthropological Association.

Arlene L. Mandell, a retired English professor from William Paterson University in Wayne, New Jersey, lives in Santa Rosa, California. She is an award-winning journalist who wrote medical and consumer advocacy articles for *Good Housekeeping* magazine. After spending ten years as an executive at New York City public relations firms, she received an MA from Columbia University.

Her first poem was published in the "Metropolitan Diary" section of *The New York Times* in 1989 when she was forty-eight. Since then, her essays, poems, and short stories have appeared in more than 375 publications, including *Tiny Lights*, *True Romance*, and *Women's Voices*, and in seventeen anthologies. She was the winner of a NJ Press Association Award in 1975 for a feature article, "Credit in a Man's World," and of the 2008 AAUW/CARE National "Education Is Powerful" short story contest.

She has recently published *Scenes from My Life on Hemlock Street: A Brooklyn Memoir*, which is set in the 1940s and '50s at www.echapbook. com/memoir/mandell.

Born and raised in rural Montana, **Jessie Marchesseau** grew up with the Rocky Mountains in her backyard. At the age of twenty, an avid skier, snowboarder, and mountain biker, she crammed as much gear as she could into her bright-yellow car and headed south in search of the quintessential ski bum lifestyle. All roads led to Kirkwood, California.

More than a decade later, Jessie is still exploring the Sierra, spending as much time playing in the mountains as possible. She has bachelor's degrees in journalism and interior design from the University of Nevada, Reno, and is a freelance writer, journalist, and blogger. She resides in South Lake Tahoe.

Mark Maynard grew up on the North Shore of Lake Tahoe in Incline Village, Nevada, a small town that blessed him with enough quirky characters from an early age to populate a lifetime of stories.

He left the slopes of Tahoe for the shores of the Pacific, attending college at the University of San Diego.

Mark earned his MFA in creative writing from Antioch University, Los Angeles. His short fiction has been selected as runner-up for *Our Stories'* Gordon Award and as honorable mention in the Torrey House Press Winter 2011 Fiction Contest. His work has also appeared in *Shelf Life Magazine*, *The Duck and Herring Pocket Field Guide*, the *Tall Grass Wild Things Anthology*, and the *Novel and Short Story Writer's Market 2010*. Mark is the fiction editor for *The Meadow* literary journal and lives in Reno, Nevada, with his wife and two sons where he can sometimes be found performing stand-up comedy at the Third Street Bar downtown.

Mark's first collection of short stories, *Grind*, will be published by Torrey House Press in 2012. www.markmaynard.info

Kailyn McCord is thrilled to appear in *Tahoe Blues*. Her work has previously appeared in *The Healing Muse*, *The Believer*, *Reed College Creative Review*, *The 826 Quarterly*, and online at The Rumpus. Kailyn grew up in Oakland and spent many winters in the Tahoe area with her family and friends. She left California to attend Reed College in Portland, Oregon, where she earned her bachelor's degree in English and creative writing in 2009. She lives in Portland still, works as a production assistant and stagehand at Portland Center Stage, and rides her bicycle year-round. When not working behind the scenes or writing, Kailyn spends most of her time baking bread and applying to graduate school.

John Q. McDonald is an astronomer who lives, writes, and paints in the San Francisco Bay Area. He has worked at the SETI Institute and the Smithsonian Astrophysical Observatory, and is now at

Space Sciences Laboratory at UC Berkeley. He has also worked with telescopes at Mount Laguna and Lick Observatory, and at the Canada-France-Hawaii Telescope on the summit of Mauna Kea. The experience of place, both natural and man-made, is a theme in John's creative work. He has been painting in oils and writing essays and stories since 1992. Several of his stories and essays have been published in various small journals, and he was a finalist in the 2007, 2008, and 2009 San Francisco Writers' Conference writing contest. John is currently working on two novels.

Brittany Michelson taught high school English and Spanish for several years in Arizona, and English as a second language in Ecuador. She was born in San Diego and lived there until age thirteen when her family moved to Prescott, Arizona. She moved to Los Angeles in December 2008 and completed the MFA Creative Writing program at Antioch University in December 2010.

Dave Murcar was born and raised in Spokane, Washington. He has previously contributed to *EDGE* 2010. During college he occasionally earned money performing stand-up comedy. Today, kids' events, work, and the vagaries of life keep him constantly and enjoyably occupied; yet it is a rare sight when he can be glimpsed without a novel nearby. He currently resides in Pennsylvania with his wife and four kids.

Erica Olsen lives in the Four Corners area, where she does contract archives and museum work. She has an MFA in writing from the University of Montana. Her stories and essays have appeared in *ZYZZYVA*, *High Country News*, and other magazines, and her collection of short fiction, *Recapture*, will be published by Torrey House Press in fall 2012.

Mike Pielaet-Strayer was born and raised in South Lake Tahoe. His parents bought him his first typewriter at a garage sale for thirty dollars when he was in second grade, and he's been writing ever since. He is currently enrolled as an English studies major at CSU Chico.

Brandon Pina is the author of the essay "Doohickey Fixation," which appeared in *The Kokanee* 2010, and the poem "The Mess on Boogie Street," which will appear in the forthcoming issue of *The Kokanee*, published by Lake Tahoe Community College. Brandon is a proud member of the Tahoe Writer's Block, a local writing workshop group.

Eve Quesnel has lived in Truckee, a mountain pass away from the "jewel" of Lake Tahoe, for twenty-five years. Now that her daughter is on her own, she lives with her husband and three dogs (a true Tahoe-ite owns at least one dog). Her favorite pastimes are fussing in the yard, walking in the nearby woods, hiking in the High Sierra, reading, and writing. After completing her master's in literature and environment from the University of Nevada, Reno, Eve began teaching English in Truckee at Sierra College. She also writes book reviews and occasional environmental articles for the local independent newspaper *Moonshine Ink*. Eve's essay and its epigraph appear in *Wildbranch: An Anthology of Nature, Environmental, and Place-based Writing* (2010). In 2006, she was a proofreading assistant on *Oh, Give Me a Home: Western Contemplations*, written by Ann Ronald, and she worked closely with Michael P. Branch as an editorial assistant on *Reading the Roots: American Nature Writing Before Walden* (2004). Eve has been a member of the Association for the Study of Literature and Environment (ASLE) since 2002 and writes essays for its biennial conference on the complexities and shifts between nature and culture.

Laura Read is a writer and photographer living in Northern California. Her work is published online and in national magazines and newspapers. She specializes in stories about Ireland, California, farming and food, quirky high achievers, and outlandish adventures. She's working on a nonfiction book called *Persistent Fruit: A Tale of Competition and Adaptation in the California Foothills*. She loves exploring strange and lovely landscapes by ski, bicycle, kayak, canoe, and many other forms of human-powered equipment. Most of all, she loves a great story.

Bruce Rettig is the author of literary short stories, essays, and flash fiction. He graduated from the University of Colorado with a BA in fine arts and fine arts history. In 2003, his short story "Storm Door" was the winner of the Peralta Press YK3 Contest for Best in Fiction. In 2004 he was an Honorable Mention Winner in the XVII Consecutive New Millennium Awards for "All Wired Up and No Place to Go." He's completed his first novel and is now working on a second.

Bruce lives in South Lake Tahoe, California, and works full time at his advertising agency during the day and writes fiction at night. He continues to enjoy the creative process and is one of the founding members of Tahoe Writers Works, where he works as publisher of its literary publication, *EDGE*. He helps support various arts and culture groups in the Lake Tahoe area including the Tahoe Tallac Association and its cultural events program at the Valhalla Historic Site. www.brucerettig.com

tahoe blues

Frank Riley has been singing the Tahoe blues for over thirty-three years, ever since he decided to take a summer off before applying to law school and just sort of forgot to go. His stories have appeared in *EDGE*, *The Kokanee*, *Verbsap*, and *The Fifth Di*. He has just completed a murder mystery novel set in a casino in outer space. After careers with national chain toy stores, Great America amusement parks, all five Tahoe casinos, and retail office supply, Riley happily sells stamps, and waters plants in his modest Lake Tahoe home.

Suzanne Roberts's poetry books include *Shameless* (2007), *Nothing to You* (2008), *Three Hours to Burn a Body: Poems on Travel* (2011), and *Plotting Temporality* (2012). Her memoir, *Almost Somewhere: 28 Days on the John Muir Trail*, is forthcoming from the University of Nebraska Press in 2012. She holds a doctorate in literature and the environment from the University of Nevada, Reno, and currently writes and teaches in Lake Tahoe, California. www.suzanneroberts.org

Born and raised in Tahoe City, California, **Meghan Robins** spent the majority of her childhood romping through the granite woods of the Sierra Nevada. Spoiled by high peaks and pristine lakes, she thought the rest of the world must hold even more wonderment than this alpine gem. She earned her bachelor's degree in English with a minor in philosophy at the University of Oregon, then moved to Rome, Italy, in search of romantic adventures. Two months later she found herself in southern Spain working on a farm, tilling the land while fending off an aggressive alpha goose and an overly randy turkey. After weeks of averting birds and their respective intentions, Meghan got a job at an elementary school in a tiny village south of Madrid. She quickly learned their thickly accented version of Castellano, and every day she ran along *la ruta* de Don Quixote.

When the school year ended, she left the agrarian land of central Spain for the majestic topography of New Zealand, where the mountains are fearless, the people are genuine, and the lakes are a foggy yet brilliant turquoise. Although gigantic ferns and jagged peaks rival the beauties of her own tromping grounds, she knew it was time to return home. Now she spends her days writing, using an array of styles from historical fiction to futuristic, all while enjoying every moment she lives in the unparalleled mountains of Lake Tahoe.

Ryan Row is currently a student at Lake Tahoe Community College. He is studying English to transfer. He works in a little liquor store. He is heading where he is heading about as fast as anyone else. He has been published in the *The Kokanee*, *Not About Religion*, and the *Writings on the Wall* anthology.

June Sylvester Saraceno is author of *Altars of Ordinary Light*, a collection of poems published by Plain View Press, as well as a chapbook of prose poems, *Mean Girl Trips* by Pudding House Publications. Her work has appeared in various journals including *American Journal of Nursing*, *California Quarterly*, *Common Ground*, *Ginosko*, *The Haight Ashbury Literary Journal*, *The Pedestal*, *Poetry Motel*, *Quicksilver*, *The Rebel*, *Silk Road*, *Smartish Pace*, *Southwestern American Literature*, *Tar River Poetry*, and *The Rambler*; as well as three anthologies: *A Bird as Black as the Sun*, *California Poets on Crows and Ravens*; *Intimate Kisses: The Poetry of Sexual Pleasure*; and *Passionate Hearts: The Poetry of Sexual Love*. Originally from Elizabeth City, North Carolina, she is currently a professor and English Program chair at Sierra Nevada College in Lake Tahoe where she is founding editor of the *Sierra Nevada Review*.

Sherry Sellars grew up in Los Angeles but has lived in Northern California most of her adult life. After traveling throughout Europe, Mexico, Central America, and the Caribbean, she tried settling down—first in Calaveras, then Humboldt and Mendocino counties. Instead, she married her husband and moved to the South Lake Tahoe area. Inspired by the beauty of the Eastern Sierra and the local writing community, she is currently working on a collection of essays and short stories and plans to stick around for a while.

Steve Shilstone is an elderly hippie-lite loon. He has unloaded trucks and worked stock for a department store, coached baseball, distributed mail, painted pictures, and written stories. His baseball novel, *Chance*, was published in 1996. Presently, four of nine stories in his children's fantasy e-book series, *The Bekka Chronicles*, have been released by Wild Child Publishing (www.wildchildpublishing.com). He is seeking a publisher for his 1970s child-of-hippies novel, *JC*.

Originally from the Bay Area, **Melissa Siig** is an award-winning writer based on the North Shore of Lake Tahoe. She started her writing career as a staff reporter for the *Tahoe World* after moving to Tahoe in 2001. Previously, Melissa had lived in Washington, DC, for six years where she went to graduate school for Middle East politics and worked in the government, foreign affairs, and defense consulting. She traded her high-powered career for a beautiful, balanced life in Tahoe, where she has been freelancing for the last six years, in addition to working as an editor and reporter for *Moonshine Ink*, a local monthly newspaper. Melissa's articles have appeared in *Alaska Airlines Magazine*, *Ski*, *Skiing*, ESPN.com, *Reuters*, *Reno Gazette-Journal*, *Nevada Magazine*, *Tahoe Quarterly*, *Backcountry*, and *Sierra Heritage*. She lives in Alpine Meadows with her husband, Steven, three children, and one cat. In addition to journalism, Melissa enjoys hiking, biking, skiing, and yoga, and blogging about her life at www. mountainmommamusings.com.

Gloria Sinibaldi has spent the majority of her career working in the field of employment. Along with raising three children and seeing them through college, she worked for the Employment Development Department. There she helped many to find work and achieve self-sufficiency. She coordinated PRONET, a 250-member professional job club. For this effort she received a Sustained Superior Accomplishment Award. She also coached welfare recipients in job search skills, strategies, and self-esteem. As a trainer she traveled throughout California instructing EDD employees in job service outreach. Beginning in 2001, her focus changed to unemployment insurance. At the EDD Adjudication Center in San Francisco, she managed a team preparing them to process and adjudicate unemployment claims. She has done extensive community outreach on behalf of her clients and in support of small businesses in the Bay Area and in Lake Tahoe where she has resided with her husband, Ralph, since 2006. At South Tahoe High School, she taught job search skills to special education students, including the severely handicapped. Now retired, she continues to help others by offering résumé assistance to those in need. She began writing as a child in her hometown of San Leandro, California, where she submitted stories to the *Oakland Tribune*. These were published, giving her encouragement to keep writing. She has pursued her passion for writing by taking courses through UC Berkeley and Lake Tahoe Community College. Additionally she attended Ohlone College in Fremont and earned a Certificate of Human Resource Management through UC Berkeley Extension.

tahoe blues

Paul Sohar came as a young refugee from Hungary to the United States. With a partial scholarship he managed to get a BA in philosophy at the University of Illinois and a day job in the research lab of a drug company. He was hoping to pursue literature on the side until he hit the big time, but it was only after he quit and went on disability that the trickle of his publications began to swell— eventually to over two hundred (*Agni, Chelsea, Kenyon Review, Partisan Review, Rattle, Seneca Review*, etc.) and seven books of translations, starting with *Maradok-I Remain*, an anthology of Transylvanian-Hungarian poets (Pro-Print, Romania, 1997). This was followed by *Dancing Embers*, selected poems by the Hungarian poet Sándor Kányádi, published by Twisted Spoon Press, Prague, 2002. More recently a volume of his own poetry finally appeared (*Homing Poems*, by Iniquity Press, 2005). His latest book is a prose work: *True Tales of a Fictitious Spy*, creative nonfiction about the Stalinist gulag system in Hungary. His stage credits include the musical *G-d Is Something Gorgeous*, produced in Scranton, Pennsylvania, in 2007; he wrote the lyrics and collaborated on the book. He also acts as an outside editor for a Hungarian literary journal, selecting American poets for translation and publication. He writes the introduction to each collection. He is also the translator of a Transylvanian-Hungarian bestselling author, Zolán Böszörményi; *Far from Nothing*, the first result of their collaboration, was published by Exile Press in Toronto. He has been an invited speaker at MLA conferences.

Jeanine Stevens has graduate degrees in anthropology and education. For many years, she taught at American River College, and was newsletter editor for the California Postsecondary Education Commission and the California Department of Transportation.

Jeanine has three Pushcart nominations and poetry awards from the Stockton Arts Commission, the Mendocino Coast Writer's Conference, and the Bay Area Poet's Coalition. She was awarded the 2009 Ekphrasis Prize for "Frida in a White Dress." Her chapbooks have been published by Finishing Line Press (*Caught in Clouds*), Poet's Corner Press (*The Meaning of Monoliths*), Rattlesnake Press (*The Keeping Room*), and the Indian Heritage Council (*Boundary Waters*). *Eclipse*, a "little snake broadside," was published by Rattlesnake Press.

Her poems have appeared in *The South Dakota Review*, *Poet Lore*, *Poetry Depth Quarterly*, *Tiger's Eye Journal*, *Ekphrasis*, *EDGE*, *Sierra Nevada Review*, *West Wind*, *Alehouse*, *Quercus Review*, *Pearl*, *Centrifugal Eye*, *Valparaiso Poetry Review*, *Tipton Poetry Review*, *Desert Voices*, *PMS poem-memoir-story*, and *Poesy*, among others.

Her photographs and essays have appeared in other publications. Jeanine was raised in Indiana and now divides her time between Sacramento and Lake Tahoe. In addition to writing, she enjoys traveling, tai chi, Balkan folk dancing, and hiking in the Sierra Nevada.

A native Californian, **Suzanne Stone** fell in love with the mountains at a very early age. In her youth, she spent every summer vacation exploring the High Sierra with her extended family. She has been a resident of South Lake Tahoe for many years. During that time, she has written for almost every periodical published in the Tahoe Basin. She has been a feature writer, business reporter, local columnist, and correspondent for the area. When she first came to Tahoe, she ran a campground for visitors. She has taught at Lake Tahoe Community College and Western Nevada Community College. In 1997, she received the Outstanding Teacher: Nevada Governor's Literacy Award.

In addition to writing, Suzanne enjoys playing the cello with two local groups: Sierra Strings of Tahoe and Dream Spirit Baroque Band. For pleasure, she spends many hours hiking and kayaking in the Tahoe Basin.

Janice Wilson Stridick's poems, essays, and stories have been published or are forthcoming in *Arts & Letters*, *Atlanta Review*, *Coachella Review*, *Monarch Review*, *Philadelphia Stories*, *New York Arts Magazine*, *Studio One*, *Schuylkill Valley Journal*, *US 1 Worksheets*, and other venues. Her writing has been nominated for a 2013 Pushcart Prize, and her chapbook chosen as finalist for the Arts & Letters PRIME Poetry Prize. Between 1975 and 1980, she worked at Harveys Resort Hotel as a cocktail waitress and lived in a tiny, butane-heated cabin at Zephyr Point. On September 4, 1980, she swam across the lake and then returned to the University of California to resume her flatland life. She now lives in a renovated, fully heated Queen Anne Victorian in her home state of New Jersey with her delightful architect-husband and one cranky cat. She has an MFA in writing from the Vermont College of the Fine Arts.

Karen Terrey teaches English and creative writing at Sierra Nevada College in Incline Village, Nevada. She offers writing workshops in Truckee, California, through her business Tangled Roots Writing, and serves as poetry editor for *Quay*, a literary arts journal. Her poems have been published in such venues as *Moonshine Ink*, *Sierra Nevada Review*, *Autumn Sky*, *Word Riot*, *Rhino*, *EDGE*, *MeadoW*, *Wild Apples*, and *Flyway*. She earned her MFA from Goddard College and is the recipient of a Sierra Arts Endowment Grant in 2009 and a John Woods Scholarship to the Prague Summer Program. www.karenaterrey.blogspot.com

Liz Tucker is a writer of both fiction and poetry and a graduate of the San Francisco State University creative writing program. Her short stories can be found in *Transfer Magazine*, and she was a runner-up in the WOW! Women on Writing Spring 2011 Flash Fiction Contest. Her poetry can be found in the *Red River Review* and the 2011 issue of *The Aroostook Review*. Liz continually seeks new lines whether in free-heel skiing or surfing, a new line on parenthood, and, yes, new lines on the page. Liz is a sixth-generation Californian living in Truckee, California, with her husband and two children. When she is not writing, she can usually be found anywhere outside. www.liztucker.wordpress.com

Lisa Veyssiere's poetry and short fiction has been published in the *Salt River Review*, *Ascent Aspirations*, and *Word Riot*. She is the poetry editor for *The Tonopah Review*, www.tonopahreview.org, a journal of Great Basin poetry and fiction.

Duane Wallace moved to South Lake Tahoe in 1974 at age twenty-one to open a steak house. He left Fresno State to take advantage of the opportunity to go into business. He operated a second restaurant in Carson City, Nevada, from 1980 to 1990. He owned those businesses for sixteen years. In 1991, Duane became a commercial real estate agent; he was also an adjunct faculty member and taught business and personnel classes at Lake Tahoe Community College. Duane served as the CEO of the Chamber of Commerce from 1994 to 2006, as an elected official of the South Tahoe Public Utility District for four terms, and as a school board member. Duane was also the executive director of four Boys and Girls Clubs and a teen center. He was the original founding secretary of the Reno Tahoe Winter Games Organizing Committee. Duane was also appointed by the US Secretary of Agriculture to the Federal Advisory Committee, reporting to the White House on the Tahoe environment. Duane is a graduate of the US Chamber of Commerce Institute for Organizational Management conducted at the University of San Diego.

When I Asked Mom Where I Came From, or a Very Brief Biography
August 1945

World War II in Europe was through, and Tojo was still playing hide and seek in the Pacific. Master Sergeant Francis James Ward, a native of Bayonne, New Jersey, aka The Jersey Kid—a dub garnered in wartime Italy—had just been honorably discharged from the USAF, having survived twenty-four bombing runs over Germany. Petty Officer 1st Class Muriel Florence Kelly, a bombshell from Brooklyn, was still enlisted in the WAVES.

Somewhere in the Irish Catskills

Across the room a brassy quartet blows a lazy version of "Sentimental Journey" while a brunette with a face like an Ingrid Bergman soft focus close-up, Veronica Lake peek-a-boo bangs, and red lipstick sits at a corner table with a couple of tough numbers smoking a Pall Mall and drinking Rheingold out of a pilsner glass.

"Hey Kel," Marion says, "check the flyboys what just walked in. That one in the bomber jacket's something like—wouldn't ya say?'

My jaw dropped and I just says, "Ohhhh Marion."

"Jesus, Kel," she says, "he's coming over." It was your father. So he comes over and gives me his silly line of malarkey, and I fell for it.

Daniel Ward was born in Bayonne, New Jersey, in 1956 on a cloudy day in October.

Pamela Warman was born and raised in Chile, but made South Lake Tahoe her home in 1995. She has been working in the ski industry ever since, where she has found a new true family. She works as a ski instructor and a ski technician during the winter and in summer tries to do the least amount of work in order to write and play in the Tahoe Basin.

Born in Montreal, Canada, **Tom Wendell** grew up near Los Angeles. Raised bilingual speaking English and German, he has visited Germany several times. He attended Catholic schools until transferring to public high school. During that time, he developed his love for bicycling, skiing, and surfing. After a semester of community college in 1969, Tom moved to Mammoth Mountain to pursue skiing and escape the smog and congestion of LA as he awaited the outcome of the draft lottery for the Vietnam War. Having narrowly missed being drafted, Tom traveled and worked in Europe for eight months.

In 1975, Tom returned to college to study psychology, sociology, and physical education. Working as a bicycle courier, he sustained an injury to his right knee that would greatly influence his future. After a stint managing a restaurant in Santa Monica, California, Tom had the first of twelve surgeries on his right knee in '78. The challenge of rehabilitating this and other injuries steered him toward expanding his knowledge of health, nutrition, diet, and exercise. His efforts paid off as he still pursues his most beloved sports and remains very fit at age sixty despite having a total of twenty-three surgeries and numerous broken bones. Being sponsored as a pro monoski instructor at age fifty was another testament to his pursuit of health and fitness.

tahoe blues

Today, Tom is on the City Sustainability Commission and is a longtime advocate for cycling and sustainability. He writes to process his thoughts and regularly contributes to local media.

Amy A. Whitcomb grew up in New England, attended college in Virginia, and spent most of her twenties looking at flowers in the Sierra Nevada of California. She returned to graduate school in 2010 after working in Sequoia and Kings Canyon National Parks and for the scientific journals *PNAS* and *PLoS ONE*. She now studies creative writing in the master's of fine arts program and environmental science in the master's of science program at the University of Idaho.

Kai White dabbles in teaching writing, consulting in historic preservation, and reviewing books, along with raising her daughter in one of the most isolated places on the planet. Currently teaching English composition at Hawaii Community College in Hilo and online for Chaminade University in Honolulu, she is writing a national register nomination for the Kilauea Lodge in Volcano Village and will pen a nature writing feature review for *ForeWord Magazine* this fall. For fun, she and her husband enter open ocean swim races in Hawaii, and hope their daughter, Clara, will soon be swimming alongside them.

Bona Fide Books is a small press on a mountaintop connecting writers with their readers.

www.bonafidebooks.com